The Same Life Twice

Frank Kuppner was born in Glasgow in 1951. He has been Writer in Residence at the universities of Edinburgh, Strathclyde and Glasgow. In 1995 he won the McVitie's Scottish Writer of the Year prize for for his book *Something Very Like Murder*. He received a Creative Scotland Award in 2003.

FRANK KUPPNER

The Same Life Twice

CARCANET

*t*ESCORIA

First published in Great Britain in 2012 by
Carcanet Press Limited
Alliance House
Cross Street
Manchester M2 7AQ

www.carcanet.co.uk

A CIP catalogue record for this book is available from the British Library

ISBN 978 1 84777 145 2

The publisher acknowledges financial assistance from Arts Council England

Supported by
ARTS COUNCIL
ENGLAND

Typeset by XL Publishing Services, Tiverton
Printed and bound in England by SRP Ltd, Exeter

The Same Life Twice
(With One Echo)

Left

1
No, there'll never be
another me! – whatever the Universe
might proceed to do next!
(At least, I bloody well hope not.
For my own sake, if nothing else.)

2
Yes. So many thrown threads
tangle together somehow or other –
each of us coming out of
such a knot! – then, in their turn,
sooner or later pulled apart.

3
I had never before
seen quite such an expression
on a woman's face – and yet,
strangely enough, I
recognised it instantly!

4
This light in the kitchen! What dazzling
insight it must have taken
for some great genius somewhere
to realise that the Sun
was in fact *not* a God!

Right

1
No. Never another vast complexifity
leading to quite this effloration –
if I may put it that way.
(And who may put it that way
if not me? Eh?)

2
So many lovely complex threads
tangled together
somehow or other –
How far back can we trace any of them?
Or forward at all? Eh? Yes?

3
"My first thought, Eve, was that
having somehow or other managed
to think out your impossibly good face –
it flashed across his mind that now perhaps
would be the perfect moment to retire."

4
"But then, Eve, I thought, having somehow
managed to add the rest of you –
that was that! Off he went,
up in a flash of warm, golden light. Which (I dare say)
is more or less where that sun there must have come from."

5

Well, yes – I too travelled
through all the ranges of Heaven –
but I can't quite remember
a single thing about it *now*!
Damn! (Or the other thing.)

6

"And what makes you think
that somebody like you
is going to be very satisfied
with the state of the next world either?
Thank *God* I won't be there with you."

7

"You know, the people who live
in the flat through that wall there
seem to spend an awful lot their time
f★★★ing. (Or are they in fact
doing something else?)"

8

By now, I have heard
two quite unrelated people say:
"Why won't they let me die?"
The exact same words too, I think.
Or certainly, very nearly the same.

9

There would be little point
in not still loving you
when I was dead, would there?
(Although, I freely admit,
it's a rather ridiculous question.)

5

In the slightly untidy kitchen
I put down the hot, slopping mug
onto the nearest available object –
in fact, a map of the Moon
given away free by a newspaper.

6

How many meals do you suppose
are being prepared even in this street
at just this moment?
Yet it seems so quiet here
beside this newly painted kitchen wall.

7

How young our parents were –
it now turns out –
when all this sort of
nonsense started
to happen to them too!

8

"Is this the last time, I wonder, Adam,
I'll ever have to send anyone
my *curriculum vitae*?
It changes all the time, of course;
though never, alas, quite enough."

9

There would not be much point
in loving you when I was dead,
would there? (Although, I admit,
it's a rather technical question.
(And if you were dead [too]?))

10
"And yet, if we ever meet again,
surely it will only be
after we have ceased to exist.
And I rather doubt if that
will be good enough for you either."

11
No, Sir [or Madam]: the dead
do not go off into darkness –
(or, for that matter, into light!)
They simply cease to exist.
(Not that 'simply' is quite the word, is it?)

[It so rarely is.]

12
And so God, with a look of some
slight puzzlement on his (of course) superb features
glanced round himself once or twice and suddenly
realised: "Oops! Oolala!
It just isn't there any more, is it, Dan?"

["But wasn't there another emptiness here already?"]

[Dear me! I hope I'm not repeating myself *again*.]

13
but so many people fall out
of more or less any clock anyway –
then pick themselves up
(or do not pick themselves up) –
[on the clocks sardonically go for all that!]
till the damn thing finally stops –

10

But if ever we meet again, my darling,
surely it will only be
after we have both ceased to exist.
And still I cannot promise you, Beatrice,
that I'll have improved quite enough [even by then].

11

And yet again, I am not entirely sure I would
have preferred to live forever. No.
(I who say that on the sheer off-chance
that anyone who overhears me
can [could] do anything practical about it!)

[Who is that? Identify yourselves!]

12

But there is next to nothing
actually there now, is there?
And yet, I wake up in the armchair
anyway. Oh, good.
Time to go to bed again!

[Which reminds me: "I wake up in the comfortable chair / which I
remember once seeing my mother / suddenly wake up in herself / maybe
twenty years ago now. / And it's such a lovely, bright afternoon!" (Which,
if I may honestly say so, actually happened on the very day this work was
first brought to a form of completion [29j10]! Thank God [I, he] one
revises.)]

13

Well, yes, I've had my life.
Or whatever the f★★★ it was.
No-one can take it from me now.
Mind you –
who would ever want to? Eh?

14
Who has never
been at all struck by the fact
that dead bodies
can look so exactly like living bodies
(for a while at least?)

15
Oh, well – maybe we'll break through
to something else after all.
Maybe even something higher,
whatever *that* might mean. (But, no.
No. That probably won't be us.)

16
"But if I should suddenly drop dead, Eve,
I rather trust that most of my real friends
will know what work of mine to destroy *pronto*
and what to preserve with care and love –
no doubt for the splendid edification of future ages."

[A pleasantly common fantasy, I suppose.]

17
Stoically, the gradual process
of wise deterioration continues –
(or not so gradually) –
But isn't it marvellous? No?
(No? Isn't it *still* marvellous?)

18
These days I am doing
some of the best work
I have ever done.
(I think.)
(But how much does that matter, darling?)

14

Odd, to have a life that finishes
without ever having quite
got finally started.
(I must simply have assumed that people
would be a bit more interested.)

15

What! Was that my life?
That really was my life, was it?
I don't believe it!
Isn't there some specific office somewhere
that I can go and complain to?

16

God, but I can remember
so many [tiny] mistakes!
Have I really lived so long? Most of the time
I feel immortal – but I dare say
[that's just another of my mistakes!]
that's one of my more serious ones –

17

So. We all emerged from small,
miraculous but vulnerable openings,
to kill each other – (or it may be love) –
and meanwhile even deduce some things correctly
about, for instance, our sudden[ly] neighbouring stars.

18

What a thing to be able to do!
Imagine – the Universe has managed
to get mere material to behave like you! –
(and, at least just as strange, like me!) –
[and, perhaps even stranger, like me!]
to get all this here, having these superb thoughts –

19

Blessed indeed is he
who, by a magnificent exertion
to the fullest extent of his powers,
can just manage to keep himself
a very small step ahead of his public!

20

To the people of Maryhill
I said more or less nothing –
no, nor they to me.
Well, Eve, they were often drunk –
and I was usually in hiding anyway.

21

What? Have I really never written
a line in this big front room before?
(it seems so unlikely!) –
after so many successful moments
speaking here on hundreds of mornings! –

22

Wakening up, to find myself
in the wrong room entirely.
I don't know. In the end,
I suppose I don't really want
not quite to be obsessed by women.

[But doesn't 'obsessed' mean: / 'thinking too much about'? Yes? / How
then, Eve, / could I possibly be obsessed by you – / (or, indeed, by, erm,
women in general?)]

19

"What the world most needs now
is a towering, overwhelming genius
who is willing to tell it exactly
what it most wants to hear! (And, alas, Dang,
you fall down badly here on one count at least.)"

20

"And now, if you would, Master,
kindly give us again the benefit
of some of your sublimer
insights – only, this time, please,
with all your false teeth back in place."

21

Such spirituality!
The absolutely highest way
of not being honest.
(But it's probably about time
to climb down from the kitchen table.)

22

"Good morning, darling. Where
are all the necessary adjectives
when most you need them? Beautiful
day, isn't it? Beautiful. (And I would so gladly
say so much more. But language has failed me again!)"

[I doubt, Dain, whether anyone / really wants to be told / that he's
obsessed by ★★★★. / (And that's such an ugly word, / isn't it – 'obsessed'?)]

23
Oh! Everyone lying in (his or) her bed
suddenly fell out of his (or her) bed –
onto the individually accepting floor!
Or perhaps onto some sort of soft, yielding surface?
Astonishing, at any rate! (Yes. [Whose key is this?])

24
Yes! Powered it seems by the batteries
of these small intricate sexual details, I
shall rise into a sort of stratosphere
above even the routine roof of this
in fact highly desirable almost-city-centre flat!

25
Clouds! Clouds!
Get out of my way!
She's going to talk to me!
How could anyone with body hair
ever hope for quite so much?

26
This subtle smoke seeps out
of the universe, towards –
well, towards what?
Towards the top-floor flat
[where I was perhaps born?]
where I was born, perhaps?

23
Through extensive personal observation
I have, I think, established
that women are a little
different
from me[n].

[See, darling? It really is poetry after all! (As if that matters ...)]

24
These days, I just love to sit here
on most mornings, with my cup of familiar tea;
listening to my girlfriend while she –
[can this really be *someone else* too?]
(and yet – oh, no! – just a moment!
Maybe this really is *someone else*?)

25
So here we are then: all of us,
carrying so many bones around
along with the shopping.
Occasionally stopping to complain about
[the *ridiculous* price of some things these days!]
the ridiculous *price* of some things these days!

26
What do we get at best
but the briefest, most narrow glimpse
of the immediate life around us?
(And even that is so threateningly vast
that we mostly skitter away from it, terrified!)

27

I was so sorry to learn
that there are indeed no flowers
growing on the moon.
Still, at the very least, I have
heard you weeping quietly next door.

[Or merely talking? Either would surely be astonishing enough.]

28

I would quite like to have been a hermit
perhaps somewhere up there in those thickly wooded hills –
no doubt expiating some crime,
or some major mishap, presumably involving
a woman – or, with luck, more than one woman.

29

In the empty house
he sits reading a newspaper
which tells of the outbreak
of a war no-one knows about –
while elsewhere many doors [open and] shut.

30

All this vast complexity in infinite directions!
even the single hardly fathomable cell
needed many millions of years –
while now some of us blow other human beings up
for such dull mulish gold impossible wor(l)ds!

[Yes. The thats of which we are constituted have been parts of innumer-
able other [beings] things – will scatter and become parts of innumerable
more other things which [do] did not think for a moment they were not us
– asking a few million questions in a brief, deep, fleeting glued-together –
But wait a moment! Wait a moment! I was forgetting that I am no longer
quite in an alternative Universe! (As one so often does. (But then, who
ever is *really*? How could anyone really ever be there?)]

27

Oh, why could the whole Universe
not simply have been some sort of
warm, loving orifice? I can't help feeling
(maybe it's only me?) that it missed
such an absolutely wonderful chance there!

28

"Looking at these trees, Eve,
I find I am often strongly reminded somehow
of older [other?] women's genitalia.
Hmm. Perhaps I should spend less time
round at the back of [the house] our new villa?"

29

Still. I'm quite glad not to be
another person, living
in another, different time or
a completely different place. No. Well –
that's my opinion anyway.

30

No. What matters most
is to say real things
about real things which are worth discussing.
(And not to drench the whole damn place
in wonderfully high-class historical piss.)

[Eh, Father? 'Hysterical piss' surely? – if we absolutely must have such gross
lapses in taste. ('To my eye, sometimes the entire Universe resembles
nothing so much as a gross lapse in taste.' (*Bradley*.)) (Not *that* Bradley, of
course.)][Rhetorical?]

31

So. Somehow they got to know each other;
were happy or unhappy – or, variously, both –
and soon enough departed, usually in boxes;
and we, who shall (of course) be here forever
may at times perhaps summon up a mild interest in whatever
       the f★★★ it was that they may quite have managed to do.

32

Sitting down for a breather
at surely the remotest bench
in this whole rugged plantation wood,
I notice, in the nearby wastepaper basket,
a copy of this morning's newspaper.

[Planegg, I suppose?]

33

That strange feeling one has sometimes, Eve –
almost as if one were reading the wrong book.
Not that it's bad exactly, no –
in fact, it's certainly entertaining enough.
It should just be another book, that's all.

34

The sudden, displaced ant running across your book
is one more actual item in and of the universe –
much like the deft clip from your well-bred, elegant hand
which takes its shape smartly back out of the universe again,
as such, Eve – never even suspecting so little or so much.

31
Add to the richness, O my rare children! [Or
whatever you are!] Do what you can to add to it.
If it all must flow on past,
then at least help it to do so
as richly as possible[, O my fellow deviations]!

32
Yes! There it is
in the book of old local photographs –
this house! – the very same building
in which we are now seated, heads almost
touching, right beside each other on the couch.

[Or, alternatively: Looking at a huge big book / of 19th-century photo-
graphs / before taking it back to the library – / I suddenly remember: / I
must get my watch fixed! (But I don't believe that for a moment.)]

33
Waking up from yet another brief snooze,
(in which I'd been dreaming about my first school) – (but why?) –
I glance down hurriedly at a heavy, tilting art book
which I find I have not yet quite let drop. Those clouds!
Those golden trees! Those shamelessly naked Goddesses!

(Claude? After all, I so *love* Claude. (It *is* him, isn't it? Naked goddesses?))

34
In the dead boy's room, Paris,
they have left everything (they say) just as it was –
except for a favourite photograph
once pinned above the bed
of a couple of girls (sisters?) pretending, it seems, to be [twins] cats.

35

For a moment there, my darling, I once again thought
there really was someone moving
up at that small high window just across the road.
But it was only weak sunlight, I suppose. And some glass.
Yes. An effect of trees and a slightly too quick hope.

36

But the lights! The stars. The dark windows!
one just knows that other people
are – what, Adam? – er, sorry: are *working* away
to great advantage in many of the rooms
of this not quite trivial, not quite central – what? – street.

37

Oddly enough, a cat crawling along
up there just across the road
behind a slightly raised roof-top sign
written in a widely-spoken language
which, I'm sorry to say, I don't really understand either.

38

But what do I still remember from that brief trip?
A rich, long orange mat in a small hotel.
The false teeth of a barely middle-aged translator.
Light rain falling from a bright sky
for a strangely long time. And at least one other thing, yes.

[Such an easy trick really.]

35

Only on the very morning of my departure
did I discover there was a large stain
on the pillow, underneath the pillow-case —
where my head had been placed in sleep
every night for the previous week or so.

36

I wake up in a chair in the small room —
having dreamt that I was sleeping
in the bed beside the chair where I am seated.
It's where I slept last night, as a matter of fact.
But I'm not quite over there just at the moment.

37

The sound of people talking
in different languages
on either side
of my cheap hotel room — while I
am thoughtfully silent for a while inside a third.

38

The insane sense that other countries
somehow can't really mean it!
Why do you even bother? Eh?
Who are they trying to kid?
The real thing? Where *I* am from! (And only that!)

[Billions to one against every particle of every last detail.]

39
A fly walking over a carpet!
No, really. There is just
no excuse for that sort of thing!
(Somehow Heaven now seems
even less enticing than before.)

40
On the darkening road,
an animal which no-one
has ever properly seen
runs stealthily towards
[is running unsteadily towards]
the nearest [fairly] large city.

41
As if – somewhere out of sight – a vague great lurking power
were trying to bring me personally in out of the dark
to a dazzling success! Yes! Why did it take so long for me
to grasp that this crazed belief was quite unjustified?
(Erm. If [Beatrice, in fact] it is.)

42
Not fear of death – No, Be.
But the sense that the playing days
of one's earthly career are [nearly] over.
And that one is merely hanging around
[needlessly] cluttering up the space.

39

"A rather wonderful place, yes, it was.
And yet, while I was there, wherever I went,
I invariably used to meet people –
usually such beguiling people too –
who clearly wished they were living somewhere else."

[This one – like not a few others here – could pretty well be called *Life*,
could it not?]

40

Those huge, huge blown-up photographs
of some immensely larger
distant stellar episodes –
[unexpected] on the walls of the Art Gallery
when we nipped in for a coffee!

41

Look at his or her lovely clean skull
here in its museum case! Ancient, yes –
but still with such perfect ranged teeth!
What? Some assault on a vanished heart?
Or a wrong first step into our dangerous waters?

42

Well, yes. Yes. We do study these people –
but (look!) they have all failed and even *died* –
and that's really just not
quite the sort of thing
we're ever going to descend to ourselves, is it?

[Every age is uniquely impressed by its own deaths. Look! The real thing at
last – and [it's because] we are doing it! As if all the earlier ones had been
deficient somehow; inadequate, poor imitations, not quite the real thing. I
mean to say, they're all dead already, are they not?]

43

"I am old, Helen. And there is still
so much I don't even remotely f***ing know.
But it hardly matters very greatly now, does it?
And we aren't dead yet, anyway, are we?
What? No; I thought not. So. Who's your peculiar friend?"

44

"Many of us wander around here, O Millionth Dan,
for instance, balancing clods of earth on our heads
because of what some remote idiot
once whispered long ago not even
in the world next to our own hearing – "

45

"After the moment of insight, darling,
the moment of forgetting quite what it was.
You know, I can't even remember
if somewhere I've maybe already
written this one down as well."

46

"No, it can't be that.
No. Very few poets
are ever going to teach you
anything you can learn much from.
They just don't know enough, Eve. That's all."

47

And why should anyone understand
anything, Beatrice? It's amazing
we don't all just disappear
up into the not very clear blue light
of our own eternal ignorance.
["Speak for yourself, dear."]

43

And all this ancient wisdom
so carefully compiled and preserved –
is in fact the product of baffled minds
who were guessing as they passed through
and had, by and large, Eve, very little idea –

44

"Write it down, O Thousandth Dan,
as soon as the thought strikes you.
For, however brilliant the phrase is
the chances are
you won't remember it for long."

45

"You know, this is exactly the sort of thing
I might have written myself, I think –
if only had I been
[as completely devoid of talent]
quite as displaced from reality
as was the inspired author in question here."

46

"Yes, Sir.
Yes, I have now read your latest book.
And I must say there was one comma in it
that I did so very particularly admire.
Your own, I hope?"

47

Basically, my dear Eve, we are the results
of God knows quite how many inspired blunders
other things have been making up until now.
(Oh, the occasional success too, I suppose.
If you absolutely *have* to call it a 'success'.)

48

"Dear God! All this thankless struggle
just to bring idiots up to the mighty everyday height
which I already more or less
take completely for granted. A matter of mere routine.
Hardly seems worth the effort sometimes, does it, dear?"

["But such a rare privilege nonetheless, dear Mr Swanovan, yes, to be
allowed to peruse this work of yours before it becomes dulled and, yes,
almost *ruined* by the slow, relentless infestation of crudely flushed out and
celebrated *quotes*."]

49

Later on – still that same night –
I thought I heard a knock at the door –
but I ignored it! Fool that I am –
I wish so much now that I hadn't –
but I did. (Didn't I, my darling?)

50

Once, on a tree-lined path near Munich,
a little way past a small monument to
a former local extermination camp,
I heard what must have been a window slam shut
somewhere behind a fence, among the gently swaying branches.

51

I return to the room
which I had to leave so hurriedly
several days ago.
Nothing seems to have been moved.
No. Absolutely nothing, it seems, has even been touched.

48
And what then is the good?
What? Look, Adam: just do it –
and if it isn't all that good,
then trust that, you know, [Evelation by] natural selection
will filter it out for all of us quickly enough. Okay?

[Hmm. Something of a brief dialogue on ethics, this one – though not
particularly in the Greek style, I suppose. (Aha! The Eternal Feminine!)]

49
She shut the outside door right in my
face – but soon I could hear her
weeping far off beyond it. What?
Did she somehow imagine
I had already gone? (Hmm. Or not?)

[Have we not had this already, Master?]

50
All things are illusory –
including even the deepest grief, of course.
However, most unfortunately,
those of us who have sunk into grief
are usually just a bit too obtuse to realise this.

51
I'm tired of life, she once said to me.
And even if it isn't life, she said,
I'm tired of it anyway, Adam.
Do you really think this is all there is?
Please God there won't be even more!

52
Look! A thick layer of dust
lies over half the terrestrial globe
which has been standing untouched surely for months
beside that metronome
at the top of [your] my neglected bookcase!

53
How odd –
all these inadequately motivated stars!
Are people perhaps drinking themselves to death
(just like that rather charming man next door, I suspect)
on a scatter of the other planets too? [And if not, why not?]

54
I do hope I never have to tell you, Yves,
that the spacious shower you have just used
was installed last year by a very pleasant man
who – unless something extremely odd has happened –
will pretty certainly have died of [stomach?] cancer by now.

55
Odd. Having a routine drink
of water from the tap
in a friend's house seems – (much like
performing an obscene act there, Eve?) –
so inescapably *different* somehow!

52
Listen. If the worst comes to the worst
then the worst comes to the worst –
and, if it doesn't, it doesn't.
One need not go very far
for even a whole planet to become invisible.

53
What a gross absurdity it is –
to have so much of the surface
of the necessary planet covered
by a vast, floppy and, these days
at least, profoundly inconvenient liquid!

54
Look! That unknown, unrecognised car
has been right there dead outside this window
parked on the exact same selfish
antisocial, view-obstructing spot
for the past two full weeks now!

55
A very early Sunday stroll
through a foreign wood, then down a street
of unknown, newly built houses –
on the balcony of one of which
a glorious woman sits, leafing through a newspaper.

[Well, she seemed glorious. Only a glance, of course.]

56

"I only hope my dear [ex-]husband
(while he is abroad on business)
doesn't yet again show to anyone else
any of the photographs of certain objects in this room
which he always takes with him, as he says, for company."

["Have I ever in my life / seen anything even lovelier / than these cherry
blossoms / here in Fukuoka? / Hm. Yes. Well. Once, perhaps…"]

57

Of course, I have always particularly liked
this gaunt room in a favourite neighbour's house
since a lively daughter of his (now married – now abroad)
once flashed (only the once!) her little white underpants at me
in here, with a strange, cold smile, well over ten years ago now.

[A life of heroic achievement, obviously. Incidentally, the Trojan War is
usually reckoned to have lasted ten years. (Assuming it ever really
happened, of course.)]

58

"But since, Adam, as far as I know,
she is not even quite sure where this street is,
how can she ever hope to guess that I
have been walking round this room for much of the morning
with an item of her clothing balanced precariously on my head?"

[Ah! The great existential questions! Am? Are? Is?]

59

Standing out on the balcony, [Aeneas,]
looking down at the well-kept courtyard
it suddenly occurred to me
that I might just possibly be about
to be struck with fatal effect by a stray bullet.

56

The morning sunlight
on her neat little knickers –
and she's wearing them!
(This time she is wearing them!
How much difference it makes!)

[Hmm. Like not a few others here, this is [in its 5-7-5-7-7 syllable count]
an example of the Japanese five-line poetic form often called the *tanka*. So
much for the form. As regards content, let us perhaps not investigate too
closely exactly what might be going on here, Danchi.]

57

Ah yes, those were the days! Time after time
that rather lanky big girl from next door
chose just the right moment for astonishing
her precarious young friend with a glimpse
of such a mesmerisingly intelligent absence.

[But then, how much of [everything – no] anything did ever really
happen?]

58

How odd it is that even ★★★★
is not a frame round the whole Universe –
and that even it cannot guarantee
our immortality. (In which case
we've just about had it, Eve, haven't we?)

[It surely cannot be difficult for even the least worldly to work out what
the word here censored is.]

59

Oh, yes – if only the ultimate truth
were (if I may say so) ★★★★-shaped!
(Maybe it even is!)
But, no. No. That would be
just *too* much to hope for, Be, wouldn't it?

60

Alas, none of these public statues
are even half as interesting
as the life on the benches beneath them!
And I suspect that remains true even
when there is no-one [sitting] there at all.

61

No. I'm glad to hear
it's exactly the sort of place
where a failed artist should live.
Can I ever become a success here, Helen?
Another nice clean trolley-bus deftly passes us by.

62

"Him, Dan? He's the sort of man
who couldn't even bring himself to scream:
'Who the f*** are you?'
at someone deftly coming in through
his window late at night."

63

But however often one sits about, watching
other people passing by – *them*, for instance –
somehow, Eve, one almost never thinks of others
discreetly looking out of the just as real windows
which one might happen to be walking by oneself. No?

60
"All mature art, Jan,
is part of the precarious endeavour
of getting men
to **** women properly.
(Legendarily difficult, I know.)"

[Surely not?]

61
From beyond those trees, the sound
of a nearby telecommunications building
being demolished! Glorious! How glorious! –
while we sit here in the park together,
not quite admitting what we think of each other.

62
"It's the old, old story, darling,
I'm very much afraid.
He loved her so much
that he ran smartly out of the house
early one morning and never quite returned."

63
"All these other people, Adam!
It's ridiculous!
There's something badly wrong with it.
And how I wish sometimes the truth
wasn't *quite* so bloody depressing!"

["Oh, I now understand what it's all about, darling.
And it's simply *far too depressing* – " etcetera.]

64

And why did I never do
any more substantial work?
Perhaps the main problem is
that I was such wonderful company
I was very rarely left alone?

65

What is the ultimate bloody point of this stuff,
thought God to himself one morning. I mean to say,
I'm just me and that's it! Is that all? Eh?
Is that really all? But – yes! I know! I'll create Woman!
Eves! That sort of thing! Whew! (My God, that was close!)

66

"One of the first things
I realised about my parents, Adam,
is that they did not seem to notice
how bad the air had become
in the room where they had been sleeping together all night."

67

Oh, for how long a time
those white clouds beyond the aeroplane
stayed in the dreadful, unignorable shape
of an utterly gigantic, head-up foetus!
Truly. What bizarre things people can believe!

68

"But if I were only a ghost
and you weren't a ghost –
or even, for that matter, vice-versa –
then one of us, Adam,
would *still* be a ghost, wouldn't – er – we?"

64

"Actually, darling, I find,
the more one understands of it,
the more pointless, if anything, it becomes –
even if, I admit, quite wonderfully –
not to say [almost] miraculously pointless. No?"

65

And God thought to Himself: "Hmm.
This Eve business may have been a *bad* mistake.
What is the *bloody woman* complaining about now?
Have I forgotten something?
No. I just don't understand it."

66

Oh, aren't you just so *clever* –
to have produced life from inside there!
Yes.
Why do we ever argue? (In fact,
how do I ever dare to argue with you?)

67

And through such a tiny, complicated
maddening, apparently inadequate
little opening too! (Inadequate?)
Oh, for God's sake, darling! Are we going
to argue about this now as well?

68

"You know, for a moment there I thought that was
our mother across the street –
even though she died – what? – five years ago now.
No, not her. No. The woman who looks like her
has just gone into (I think) that new bank on the corner."

69
My beloved said:
"I simply cannot imagine
trying to live without you."
(In fact, that was almost the last thing
I ever heard my beloved say to me.)

70
"I dare say I have f★★★ed
all the wrong people, Paris.
But then, that's life, isn't it?
Either that or *not*
f★★★ing all the wrong people."

[Romance, eh?]

71
"Still, I can't quite regret
my rather immense failure – apart
from the fact that it prevented
me from having a
completely real life, I suppose.
[But then, my dear, who does?]"

72
Almost every week in the last year or two
I walked straight past this place –
[I was born just round the corner] –
not, of course, *for a moment* realising
it was doing such fantastically successful business
printing out great bundles of counterfeit money.

[This is West Princes Street, obviously, isn't it?]

69
"Oh, to be forced to continue
with all this vexatious struggling
and labouring, even after
we have ceased to exist, Beatrice –
wouldn't that be *just like* the thing?"

70
"To understand so little –
and then die!
Or (as is my case) to understand
so much – and then *still* die anyway!
Quite frankly, B, I rather disapprove of all this."

71
No – that was it! –
that was the crucial moment –
[and you missed it!]
[and you missed it too?]
and I never even noticed it [in time]!
No. Instead, I just sat there, darling,
half-watching light [leaves] hesitate at a window.

72
Yes. Every day or so back then
I used to walk right past this place –
never even for a moment realising
that someone I would find so exquisite
could possibly be living none too happily just here.

73
Then, through the near wall, night after night,
yet more loud, as-if-incessant snoring from the chap
who was told, only a couple of weeks ago,
that he had inoperable cancer. (Or did I misinterpret
what I overheard him saying recently in the corridor?)

[No. I dare say this is the same chap as the one who appears in 54? Get
back to me on this one if I'm wrong!]

74
A distant cry of "Help me, Adam!"
on and off through some of the morning.
Or – (I do rather hope) – more probably,
a natural-mechanical noise that sounded
like a distant cry of "Help me, [Eve] Adam!"

[This probably, I think, works better without the names.]

75
"Look. I have just had a very strange letter from the authorities
advising me to 'go and take a running f★★★ to myself'.
I mean to say, this is hardly the language they habitually use,
Eve. Is it? Have I perhaps displeased someone or other
by an ill-judged remark on some form I lately filled in?"

76
Oh, every couple of years, Eve,
she wrote a profoundly
convincing suicide note – just about the time
when we had almost managed
to forget the previous one.

73

So much in my life, it seems, Eve –
like my terrible snoring –
practically never noticed
except by other people –
who were perhaps being driven mad by it!

[Ought I to feel *quite* so irritated?]

74

What on earth was that strange noise?
Not a cry for help out on the street?
Or was it perhaps rather
the gentle squeal of a new chair
resisting the arrival of my ever-increasing weight?

[Smartarse!]

75

"She talks as if everyone in this city
must somehow be related to each other –
whereas at present I still don't even know
the names of my various next-door neighbours! –
not even the one who [shrieks] shouts so much of the time."

76

"Stupidly, with a sudden longing, I
uttered a staled woman's dulled name –
well over ten years after
I had last, if I may say so, penetrated her slight sanctum.
So. What the *hell* is going on here now, Dante?"

[Obviously one of the inhabitants of the *Inferno*, I should rather think.]

77
"Oh God, Lord, yes! – yes –
how much I do so love the
gross emotional
dishonesty of women
(if that is *quite* the phrase, Eve) – "

[Severe troubles ahead, obviously.]

78
"And something else
which the world, I dare say,
is not yet quite ready for."
"What's that, Adam?"
"Oh, I can't be f★★★ing bothered repeating it."

79
I have done my best.
At least, I think I have done my best.
And, if it wasn't good enough,
then, Eve, it wasn't good enough.
But all the nonsense drifts on by anyway.

80
So – we jumped onto the sudden sledges –
and spun or slewed off in innumerable different
directions – until we reached
one or other edge of the earth, at which point
we all fell off in our own way! (God! It was fun!)

[Who should know if not you, *carissima*?]

77

"But what is the bloody point, O Thirteenth Dan,
of trying, you know – whoah! – to get to shove it into
women who are not intelligent? Eh? No.
No. Is there any inspiration even remotely like
the heart-breaking squeak and gibber of brainy women? Eh?"

[Just another such inhabitant, even more obviously. Wouldn't have
minded hearing the reply either, I must admit.]

78

"Look, Dan. I made the f★★★ing effort.
Yes. I f★★★ing went over there
again and a-f★★★ing-gain. Or what?
And what good did it ever f★★★ing do me?
Apart from maybe a few children, of course."

79

"Look. Tears flowing out of every f★★★ing house in the city –
perhaps even out of every f★★★ing room!
Some f★★★ing fluid or other, anyway.
Look, Mum! The desperate scientists
are already out early at their heroic f★★★ing work!"

80

In fact, I finished it, for all the good it did,
only some ten or fifteen seconds before
I heard your key once again in the lock.
You looked, I thought, terribly pleased about something.
But I never did quite learn what that something was, did I?

[Well? Did you?]

81

Coming back down, he negotiated skilfully
all the shaky and precarious steps
of the great ladder. (Dante? No.)
Then, striding out at the bottom,
he lost his balance and fell calamitously over.

82

Strangely enough, there was a
single ski lying for some reason in the lane
I nipped down on an impulse, coming back
from a touring exhibition of infinitely wide views
of late nineteenth-century Russia!

[So, Bella. The day of that small Sisley exhibition turns out to have been
the entire or central point of the whole Universe. Dear, sweet God!
Anything else can only be an overwhelming bonus.]

83

This insolent foreign rain is falling onto
the main runway, onto all the
narrow intersecting paths
which the plane is trundling past –
and even onto the clipped airport grass too.

84

Sitting politely beside her
in that inviting hotel lounge
while a thunderstorm raged outside –
bravely trying to work up an interest
in the usual fifth-rate literary rubbish –

[Ah! One of the problems of success?]

81

"Once I even – let me admit it! – lifted up
a pair of charmingly calculating little knickers
from her kitchen table – only to find
signs of a worryingly incoherent scribble
on one of the scraps of random paper underneath."

[An obvious fiction, I would say. Who knows: perhaps even a downright
lie. It's just the sort of thing he would do, believe you me!]

82

But why for that matter should her kettle
so specifically remind me at times
of my visits to Landsberg am Lech?
Did I ever use a kettle when I was there?
(And she has never been there at all!)

[Though who can be entirely certain where anyone else has ever been? Eh?
You perhaps? Amfroi? Danjo? *Toi*?]

83

'And this time it's for real!' –
said a neat little note left
on the small table near the door.
For real, is it? Huh. What isn't?
And it's not even signed either!

84

So, why then am I standing here,
looking at a near-empty car park
on which persistent rain is falling,
holding in my arms, gingerly,
a fairly large plastic bottle full of an unpleasant liquid?

[Ah, yes. I remember it well. Paisley, wasn't it?]

85
No. Where I really went wrong
was not stopping her in time
in that leafy museum car park.
(Unless perhaps that [also] was
the greatest moment of my life?)

[I am bound to say I strongly suspect a suppressed obscenity here. I don't
think this is just me, is it?]

86
No traffic at all
on that high raised road above
the river up there.
I look out of the window.
And all these other windows?

87
Yes, yes. I was wrong to throw out
that old handbag of yours –
I can see that now of course –
particularly from such
a ridiculously high window!

[It was only a joke. But a poor joke. I realise that now. Yes. It was a bad
mistake. Rather like the Universe?]

88
Did they really live ordinary lives there too?
Look! Cars are parked
by the side of our road
as if it were [a] normal enough [thoroughfare].
The planet falls on through the strange, ungripping sky.

85
Ha! When first she sees me
swinging (t)here from the thick branch
just outside her bedroom window –
what a massive shock she'll get!
(Assuming she notices me at all, of course.)

86
"How strange. Formerly, whenever
I caught sight of a hospital
my thought always was: "Oh well –
at least I'm not inside there, am I?"
And yet, Eve – just look where I am now!"

87
Only when the new bar of soap
somehow jumped out of the shower! –
what? It had only been a dream!
Why did it take me so long
to realise this, darling?

88
"You know, Eve, just for a moment,
those rather uncanny clouds up there
reminded me so powerfully
of what your [pubic] hair often looks like
as you get out of the bath."

[To be quite frank, this sort of thing is the utterance of a [not particularly observant] cad.]

89

"But was it absolutely necessary, Eve,
for so many of us to discover
that the earth was not the real thing –
except perhaps for the skies round it –
like a sort of over-elaborate [patented?] wrapper?"

90

What must Heaven be like? Well,
in crudely realistic terms,
a hole in the ground, I suppose –
if even that. One hole after another,
eh? (Exactly like Hell, in fact.)

["Again the nearly / ridiculous beauty of / the Inferno has drawn me back,
/ darling, from the crude little Paradise / I had drifted away to." (One of
the rejected verses.)]

91

Why are these plum blossoms
making a noise so very like cats?
Surely such behaviour
will detract considerably
from their traditional mystique, darling?

92

When I said I wished to learn
of everything she had done
before she met me,
she, alas, quite misunderstood –
and tried to tell me *everything*.

89

No, no, darling. Utterly beautiful.
I feel – what – as if maybe the depths
of outer space have somehow
been tamed a little, you know?
Oh, I *hoped* you were going to say that!

[A dialogue, I suppose?]

90

"Me? I'd think of Heaven, I suppose,
as an ever-blossoming succession
of cherry-trees or maybe plum-trees –
an unpredictable scatter of which
turned out to be utterly delightful women."

[All the same, I do wish I could be quite certain who is speaking just here.
(But again: isn't it pretty much *always* the case? I mean, in life too.)]

91

"Oh yes, Eve. I know exactly
how to talk to women –
that's how I got into this
appalling bloody mess
in the first place, is it not?"

92

No. When I said I wished to learn
of everything you had done
before you met me,
you must have misunderstood me – I meant
the *other* sort of everything!

93
"Yes. I'm sorry to have to admit to you, darling,
that your beloved father was in fact
a no-good alcoholic wastrel with a heart condition.
And in fact we were all *absolutely staggered*
when he ran off with that twin red-headed Greek dwarf."

[Surely not (auto-)biography? And hardly Wagner – though I think he
occurs somewhere or other hereabouts. Maybe it's the re-touched
rendering of a mythological scene? Or something from a TV show? Or, for
that matter, Dagmar, need one even quite choose between them yet?]

94
Man – said perhaps the greatest
of the old Greek thinkers –
is the only animal
whose penis typically
does not quite function properly.

[This may, just possibly, be a misremembering of Aristotle – but I think I
am right in claiming that such a remark has never been found in the
surviving *Corpus*. (Certainly not in anything like this form.)]

95
It is all transient –
except, just possibly, *the All*.
And all that is transient
is merely a superb symbol
of the non-Existent – isn't it, Adams?

[A mixture, I think, of Heraclitus, Goethe, and a second very great thinker
indeed. Not Adam Smith, obviously.]

93
If only it could have been
otherwise! (Or was it,
actually? I don't even
know that! For most of the time, darling,
I wasn't even looking properly!)

["Yes, Das. I do sometimes fear that even Existence itself might be an out-of-date technology."]

94
"Well, you know, Tenth Dan, oddly enough,
over the piece I have had an
absolutely wonderful time.
(How much enjoyment would I have had, I wonder,
if things had gone right for me?)"

[It's unimaginable, isn't it?
By the way, it is, I think, perhaps worth pointing out that Dan is a fairly
widespread Chinese name. But no doubt more or less everybody knows
that perfectly well already. The connection with Danzig, I trust, hardly
needs to be dwelt on.]

95
"No, Mr Smith, I wouldn't quite have said
I *enjoyed* reading your book. Even so,
I'm still slightly sorry
to have come to the end of it."
(Life, eh?)

["Yes, Sir. I read your scarcely necessary book – with a certain, I think,
justified amount of contempt. All the same, I found I was not entirely
unsorry – when, perhaps a little too eventually, I discovered – I had come
to the end of it. So then. Many thanks. Very many thanks!"]

96
We had to drag from a cupboard the fine mattress
which had been kept in there, untouched, for several years;
and slept on it for that one night –
pretty well in fact, I think, considering
what had happened so soon afterwards to the last person to use it.

[Death, yes.]

97
Yes. Gradually, the cast of the
vast, improvised farce changes completely –
and not always for the better!
(But is there an audience, Eve?)
(And, if so, which way is it facing?)

98
"Yes indeed, Dodam. On this planet here
roughly, say, 58 million years ago
a few of them were very articulate –
terribly keen on the immense value
of a proper – what do you call it? – ah, yes: education."

99
"What can I add? I was so utterly happy there.
So utterly happy. No thanks can be quite enough.
And all the various flowers which were for sale that morning
when they held a corner market beside the stairways to the school –
what real houses do you think they can have ended up in?"

100
Glancing out from a small café
not far from the flat which I recently had to quit
after staying there for nearly a decade,
I chance to notice a former next-door neighbour
stride past, looking most unusually anxious.

96

I often quite like reading
about death. It makes me feel
slightly less of a failure.
(Though, of course, a lot depends
on what particular mood I'm in.)

97

"Oh, just leave the pages where they fell, Adam!
The next wind will blow them away
soon enough. Or some
preoccupied passer-by will kick them.
Yes. One foot – thus! – thud! – after the next."

98

Oh, these things one keeps forever
cluttering up the place, for no good
reason, sheer
laziness, I suppose – (thought God, nonchalantly
throwing away pretty much all of it anyway).

99

How I wish these flowers
here in the newly re-opened Botanical Gardens
were not quite so keen to keep reminding me
of what was (as I now see it) the most wonderful
missed opportunity of my middle-aged life, Beatrist.

100

One day after another, Helen –
but what else should it be?
One morning after another.
One night after another night.
[Locking these dull doors with a dull sigh yet again.]
Yes, darling. Locking these dull doors with a dull sigh yet again.

101

I simply cannot bring myself to believe,
Penelope, that I shall never see
that lovely little foreign flat again.
And don't tell me I will! No. Don't!
I mean, what the f★★★ do *you* know about it anyway?

102

No, Eve, if I sit for slightly too long in this
café in the lane, I suspect I tend to
fall through a sort of
rent in the air – and nobody else even notices
that my chair has moved a little. Always assuming it has!

103

"Still – these days, pictures of the galaxies
no longer seem quite so foreign and forbidding
to me as they once did, Lala – for now there is in my life
a being with trembling peripheries, a quick mind and a
fairly intricate set of complex whorls of her own."

104

Still. I don't think the Sun
is quite correctly placed in the sky this morning.
Might it not be better somewhere else?
Look at how much space
there is in our kitchen, for instance!

105

No, darling. I really don't think the Sun
is too well-placed in the sky this morning.
Might it not even be happier somewhere else?
(After all, it more or less
shines out of one celestial aperture or another anyway.)

101

I simply cannot bring myself to believe
that I shall never again see that beautiful
little German flat where I used to stay.
No. Not even the terse and distinctly *peculiar* sign
that someone had pinned up at the communal back door!

102

"Oh, it seems I don't have a photo of her here,"
he said – "but just look at that!" – (wherewith he pointed
at the picture of – as I guessed – a jellyfish
on the wall behind his computer.) "So, Dan? An opinion?
Does that look fatal to you? Well? Yes? So? Does it?"

103

"However, these days, Dan, even such pictures of the galaxies
no longer seem quite so foreign and intimidating
to me, my enchanted one – one of the minor advantages
of no longer giving (if you'll excuse me) a flying f★★★
about anything very much in the distance, I regret to say."

104

"Depressed?
No wonder we get so f★★★ing depressed.
It only amazes me the stars
don't get depressed sometimes too.
I mean to say – if they could only *see* themselves!"

105

You know, darling? I really don't think the Sun
is all that well-placed in the sky this morning.
Wouldn't it maybe be better off somewhere else?
I mean to say – just look at how much free space
there is on top of the kitchen table here, for instance!

106

("You know, Adam, since I confessed to her
how more or less bafflingly beautiful
her navel is, (*for instance*) – her behaviour
has, if anything,
become *even less* predictable.")

107

"Oh well, Dan. Love as best you can I suppose
the nearest thing to the right person
until reality sets in – what else? –
Or until one (no doubt rather fortunately)
dies a little before that happens – "

108

"Still, for most of the time
we should forget or overlook the fact
that we are not going to be here forever.
After all, we still *are* here,
are we not? (Hello?)

[Should that not really be, '(Goodbye)'?]

109

"But I still can't understand
why I don't just drop dead straight away
whenever I glimpse your, erm, tongue, Eve.
It would surely be so much more reasonable.
Joy? Or simple disbelief? Or just too complex?"

[Don't they even begin to glimpse just how precarious it all is, Diedo?]

106
Yes – what a thought! –
what an utterly magnificent thought! –
But no – wait a minute – just at present
there's absolutely nobody else here on the planet, is there?
(What? No? Oh, all right then. Maybe better just forget it.)

107
No, I simply never
got anywhere bloody near it!
Nowhere near it.
(And these days I care less and less
whose fault any of it might have been.)

[Yes. Though it wasn't mine, *obviously*.]

108
All the people waiting on this old platform
have suddenly dropped down dead! Look, Adam!
But who notices them? No. What we really want
is an official apology
for the utterly *abysmal* service here.

109
"For whether reality
is an illusion or not –
it must be an illusion, Budd,
to believe that reality
is an illusion."

[Simple enough, surely. Because if reality is real, then it is an illusion to
believe that it is an illusion. Whereas if, *per impossibile*, it is an illusion, then
our beliefs, themselves being part of this illusion, are themselves illusions. I
think that's about the size of it, isn't it, Boodster? Or have I got this wrong
too? I can rely on you to tell me, that much at least I can be certain of.]

110
"Look, Eve. I don't know.
She left me only two or three lifetimes ago
and it's all far too confusing!
But couldn't you at least just
wiggle your neat little tongue about meaningfully again?"

111
Yes, darling. Yes, of course. Here and now link or
links, are linked, into elsewhere and elsewhen –
but then what else is there
for it (or them, or both) to link to? Eh? Well? I'm
perfectly open to suggestions. (Yes?)

112
But who will help us, even so, if not us?
this water that shook or shattered to and fro
for more years than any real being could possibly count!
until at last, or at last last, it produced – what? – gonads?
(Oh, all right. Not *quite* how it happened, I dare say.)

110

"Look, Eve. Anyone who bothers to say
that life is somehow not real
does not really believe
that life is somehow not real –
for why then *bother* saying it at all? Eh?"

[Oh, for God's sake – if the All is not real, then what possible meaning could words like 'Reality' have? And how then would the real / unreal distinction come into a language anyway? What would the real problem be? Nothing but unreal beings! The real world is more interesting, that's my opinion! But by all means ignore me if you really wish.]

111

"Or perhaps non-Existence itself
is, at its highest, merely
some sort of partial aspect
of the supreme Good? Eh?
[Had you thought about that, Dear?]
Or maybe *not*?"

[Hmm. Have you given much thought to the possibility of simply shutting up?]

112

"And after all that difficulty
in getting up onto the high wire
in the first place, Ding – it turns out
it's just so very easy
to fall off the bloody thing straight to one's death!"

113
Like ill-trained parachutists
the poets drop up towards the planet
one by one – and usually miss it
completely! Still, Dan, you have to do
the best you can, don't you? (Or don't you know?)

114
"And as for all those lectures
I have been to (or, indeed, occasionally delivered)
during a longish life –
can I now remember, to be plucked from all of them,
a single memorable thing that anyone ever said?"

115
"But of course I can remember
what I just happened to be doing
on the very day the local university
was burning to the ground. After all, Eve,
it was me who f***ing set fire to it in the first place!"

[You know, Wagslog, the comparatively straightforward truth is, I have
also seen this poem given with the conclusion: "I was in fact / doing my
damnedest to establish a decent alibi." (At least, I *assume* it must still have
been this same poem.)]

116
A vast vast auditorium –
with only a single chair (I think)
set somewhere in the middle of it!
(Or is it even in the middle?)
(Well, for that matter, Master: is it really a chair at all?)

113
Like ill-trained parachutists
the poets dropped down towards the planet
one by one – and usually missed it
completely! Still, Poshkin, you have to do
the best you can, don't you? (Or don't you? No?)

["Dropped down" is an intensive here, is it? Certainly it's hard to see how
else one might drop but downwards.]

114
"Oh God, yes. Having spouted pernicious rubbish
to innumerable poor students over several decades –
old Ludo is now able, having honourably retired,
to nurse a visceral hatred of the even better-off
during the endless cruises he must take for the good of his health."

115
"Oh, do please pardon me, my Angel –
while perhaps I fall to the ground
clutching at my heart. After all,
one has to clutch at something.
(And the proper straws aren't always available.)"

116
Brilliant, Master!
Brilliant! Unfortunately,
it was hardly worth doing at all,
was it?
Has no-one really ever told you this before?

117

Just beside the bed on which
my grandmother died ten years ago
I gently place a little picture.
It is not a picture of her. No. No, it is something
she would quite possibly never have understood.

118

I now suspect I shall never find
a book of poetry nearly good enough
to deserve to be the place, my good angel,
where I could keep safely hidden away
these priceless photographs of your incomparable wings.

119

"Oh, billions of them have come and gone by now –
without *the least idea*, Dani – no accurate idea –
of how their bodies so intricately worked!
All the non-humans, yes – other side now, please! –
and not too many of the humans either! Eh?"

120

Today, Lord, for the first time in my life,
I wondered: Might I even be dying?
But later on, hearing
the girls shouting next door,
I paid a furtive visit to the Co-operative Bank instead.

117
No, I've never read
the old fool's book: *What Is Art?*
Why bother? At best,
It could only be a superfluous, long-winded way
of suggesting the word '——'.

[Of course, 'intimating' would be a much better word here.]

118
"I found your *absolutely staggering* book
absolutely staggering, to be quite honest, Dan.
In fact, I was *absolutely staggered* by it. Yerss.
I would like to say more, but – to be quite honest –
I'm still blindly *staggering* more or less blindly absolutely about."

119
You know, I rather suspect
that Shakespeare dying must have thought:
"This is grotesque!
Absolutely grotesque!
Doesn't the bloody Universe even know who I am?"

120
But why then should we not hear non-voice after non-voice from
        every
cemetery, ossuary, urn, crypt, sepulchre in the surviving world
(perhaps even from an occasional forgotten cardboard box?)
complaining: "Hello there? What? Why is this bloody Universe
still pretending so [un]convincingly to have no idea who I am?"

121
In that attractive foreign city
many years ago now –
across from my hotel room –
a bright lamp at a window
sometimes shining on a blue dress.

[It's not clear to me whether the blue dress was, as it were, being occupied
at the time. (I suspect not.)]

122
The vase of flowers
in the window across the road
from my Oslo hotel room
[or was it Copenhagen?]
changed more than once
during the four days I was there.

[Of course it was Copenhagen! Why pretend you don't know or can't
remember? And, more probably, it was the flowers in the vase that
changed rather than the vase itself?]

123
"Good Heavens,
Adam.
I don't think
I've ever been woken up for
quite that reason before."

124
All those people
at this very moment
bleeding in all those houses!
All those stars!
"Don't worry. We should be there soon."

121
ill in a hotel room
late at night –
the sound of someone (not farting, surely?
[do they do even that here too?])
in the room next door –
what a bloody dreadful country!

122
"Enough!" cried the Lord. "Quick! Let's gather
a few angels together. Come here, Fnurt!
And Dolly! And Phning! And Furob!
Right now – all five of you
listen to me *very carefully* please."

[Meaningless names of angels.]

123
"But I'd be delighted to prove to you,
O Ninth Dan, that Time is a mere illusion –
if only you can wait there a single further moment.
It shouldn't take long. I've done the same
often enough by now. Okay then. But first – "

124
"In fact, a really great thought
occurred to me only, oh,
an hour or so ago, Orbmourn –
but I'm afraid I was *far* too busy
to bother writing it down."

125
"No. I have no desire to escape
from the sordid reality of life, Eve –
for where else is there to go to really?
What does all our greatness pivot on but
various bodily secretions? – no, please don't! – "

126
"Oh, all right then, it doesn't exist! It doesn't really exist!
But the fact is it doesn't really exist in a different
way from the way in which all the other stuff
doesn't really exist either. All right? Got that?
There's more than one way of not being there, Dan, is there not?"

127
"Well, Eve, it's *certainly*
what I would have done myself,
if I had turned up there
instead of you
in the first place."

128
"Let's just try to keep
a sense of proportion, shall we?
At worst, Satna, it would be
appallingly evil to – oh – my [mobile] phone! –
excuse me a moment, will you? Hello? Dna! Yes?"

125

"Well, Danae – there's something
in the end so terribly embarrassing
about farting loudly in Heaven –
or so I tend to find. Yes.
Or is it perhaps just me?"

126

"Well, we are really alive here in this actual world,
Reail – so let's try to do what best we can
while we are here. (Or do you perhaps
want to do the *worst* you can?) Hello?
Where did he go to? Oh, Lord! – these f***ing spirits!"

[Yes, they can be so unreliable, can't they? That's always been my experi-
ence anyway.]

127

"With an embarrassingly loud
explosion – er, well,
what does it matter?
Have you finished those
designs for the smaller stars yet, Lord?"

128

Yes. That noise there through the wall
did sound very like someone farting.
You know, I've often rather wondered
what that chap can be doing all day, Gabriel.
Not that he could *fart* all day, of course.

[It's a quick way of insisting on our essential unavoidable physicality, Porf.]

129

Past our parked car, such a steady stream of figures
talking variously into their mobile phones!
It must surely all be so very like prayer, my darling –
except when there are unseen but palpable bodies
(as I guess there usually are) on the other end of the call.

130

"Oh, Eve, if only I instead
had been the instrument in her angelic hands!
What sublime music would I myself not have emitted?"
"Sorry? What did you say?"
"Er. Nothing. No; really, Beatrice. Nothing whatsoever."

131

As for the priceless
(bejewelled) gift of
all this emotional treachery,
darling – I – what? What?
Oh, where has he or she disappeared to now!

132

But how many people are there,
my other incomparable half,
who have never even for a moment thought:
'No. It turns out you are not
the matchless person I took you for'?

133

"God Himself? No, sorry, Love.
He's just gone out of the real world for a moment.
Out of the Omniverse, yes. You know what it's [He's?] like.
No, I'm sorry, I can't tell you exactly where He is.
[But then, who ever could?]
Oh, come on! We all have our own little reasons, don't we?"

129
but what other conceivable universe
is it supposed to be happening in? –
any of it, darling – even
the pettiest crimes, flaws and stupidities
up here among the crashing [or 'crushing'?] galaxies –

130
"Oh, Adam, I'm afraid
I've recently been very badly let down
by a man – er, not you, of course."
"What?"
"Er – well, not really a man either, in fact, I suppose.
[More of a snake, to be brutally honest about it.]"

131
"It was the woman's idea, Lord,
more really than it ever was mine."
"No, it wasn't!"
"No, it wasn't, Lord. No.
Kindly forget I ever said that."

132
"After all these decades, MacAdam,
all I can really say to women in general
is perhaps –
but no – no – why bother?
(Nearly all of them know it perfectly well already.)"

133
Do I understand it?
Do I understand what?
What?
Well, of course I f***ing understand it, Eve.
["There's absolutely no need to swear like that."]
If I can't f***ing understand it, then who the f*** ever can?

134

"But where is the rest of her, Lord?
Eh? Where is the rest of her?
Frankly, this is not terribly
impressive, even for a first effort.
Eh? You call *this here* a wife?"

135

Look! Furious sunlight
on a remote balcony –
on which there is a pair
of genuinely delightful buttocks.
[(Or perhaps three.)]
(Or perhaps not.)

[Or perhaps: 'Curious sunlight'? And 'angels' – or, for that matter, angles –
(not to mention Angles) – instead of 'buttocks'? Erm. Or feet?]

136

"I'm sorry to have to say, he's exaggerating.
No-one or nothing can in fact wither forever.
We must either, Odysseus – er, sorry, Oedipus – eventually
split into other things, or merely die. Sorry,
dear. But those are the basic, crude-as-[usual]-ever facts."

137

Even though she was near death
I am sure she knew perfectly well
what was going on in my mind.
In fact, I am more or less certain
that I even saw a warm if fleeting smile.

134

"One can easily
make rather too much of Death
and Extinction," said
the Oracle, with a sigh.
"Now, do please excuse me. I'm off."

135

the child (I presume) who is shouting
(for what distant, urgent reason?)
somewhere just beyond this German cemetery –
and all these unseen bones pointing
uncomprehendingly in this or that direction!

[A mere sketch on the spot?
Still, I suppose one could call the Universe 'a mere sketch on the spot' with
some justice, if one really wanted to. In fact, some time soon, I think I very
probably will.]

136

Such blessed days! Every so often, Abble,
my translator and I broke off from feverishly
clutching at each other's bodies
to exult at just how marvellous a gift
human language was. Yes, even our own!

[Anagram of 'Babel'. Variant of Able. Suggests 'babble'. I [un]happily leave
the rest to the ingenuity of the reader. (No doubt inadequate, but what
more can I do about that now?)]

137

"But for the rest of the night her
sister did little but make
occasional tiny sudden
heart-breaking noises
when I least expected it."

138

"What is the most memorable thing
that anyone has ever said to me
since I arrived here in Heaven? Hmm; let's see.
There's bound to be so much, isn't there? Hmm. Yes.
Look – just give me a moment or two more, will you?"

139

"Oh, I know now I should have written down
more or less every remark, Dad,
which that great mind ever made to me –
but, alas, I neglected to do so. Yes.
In fact, I recorded, in fact, absolutely *nothing*."

140

"Actually, Beatrice," whispered Almighty God –
"I don't think I've ever told anyone else this before –
but the real reason why I created this whole sublime disaster –
was that I just *knew* I would so much like hearing decent girls
using *that* word. You know? Yes. Nice clean quiet creatures like
        yourself."

141

"Oh, Dante, but this world too is all too full
of remarkable verbal artists – (did you really?) –
who win over so many by interlarding
their more routine nonsense – (did you really?) –
with brilliantly phrased nonsense – did you really not know that?"

138
"But if Life or, you know,
the Universe as such
is so exciting, eAdam,
then why am *I*
so *unexcited* sometimes?"

139
"Oh, I have far too many
real tasks to look after up here, Man,
for me to worry my pretty little head about
the infinite and the eternal. Besides which, anyway,
I still keep getting those two mixed up all the time … "

140
"So many things, Beatrice,
that I have kept as souvenirs –
and now I cannot even begin to remember
what they are souvenirs of! This – er –
this strangely shaped, living thing here, for instance."

141
I suppose I must just
have taken it completely for granted
that a great crowd of people
would be genuinely fascinated by
whatever it is I was doing. No?

142
"Quite frankly, Son, if it isn't somehow or other
about *you-know-what* – (after all, you seem to know everything) –
or, just possibly, political freedom, you know, or music –
then I'm probably not going to be
all that interested in it. Sorry."

[Sorry. That should perhaps have been 'reclusive'. H'm. I scarcely thought
free verse had undone so many.]

143
After all, if I weren't here,
and you weren't here either –
it would only be other people
doing other things, would it not?
(Yes. A good bit like now, in fact.)

144
"Oh, Adam, I used to think –
all these utterly wonderful air-breathing creatures
who (it seems) haven't the remotest idea
just how astonishing and implausible they are!
But that's true of pretty much everything here, is it not?"

145
But it astonishes me, Eve – (Does it really?) –
why I do not disappear
in an ecstatic flash
of (I suppose) golden light
whenever I glimpse your, erm – your halo, is it? –

142

"And this one here I wrote
several years ago now – it's dated –
evidently while I was waiting
for the official Housing Inspector
to arrive and look at my bedsit."

[Good Heavens! Surely this at least, Adam, could with only the minimum
degree of inaccuracy be mistaken for the actual voice of our fabulously
seductive author? No?]

143

"Look! There's another one!
Yes. And there's another one!
And, unless I'm greatly mistaken –
Look! There's a fourth! And a fifth!
Oh! If only any of them would stop and talk to us!"

144

In fact, we were strangely close just then.
Closer than usual? Was that possible?
Perhaps closer than ever?
Our eyes locked. We both knew
there were only a few [years] minutes left at most.

145

"Oh, no doubt many animals
must feel something or other
like this (or not?) all of the time, Adam –
er, Eve – but what do they ever call it?"
"Well: what *can* they ever call it, O my saint?"

146
Oh, I made my way downstairs
as quickly as I could –
and what did I find? Well.
Much what I had expected to find, I suppose.
But, this time, in flames.

[Not Heraclitus *again*!]

147
"The worst may possibly be over – but then again,
dear daughter of Deirdrenot, it may just be starting;
and what sure guarantee do we have
that we won't all drop dead
within two seconds anyway? (No. None af★★★ingtall.)"

148
Don't worry, darling.
It means nothing. I mean to say,
this world here is full of apples,
is it not?
Look! There's another one over there!

[Adam reacting to the Fall in a strikingly relaxed manner?]

149
Fortunately, the angel
landed in the neighbour's garden
with only comparatively minor injuries.
(Still, Jo, it did mean that the history
of the cosmos was somewhat, you know, jiggered.)

146

"Oh, I dare say the previous occupiers
were ecstatically happy here too –
if reports I have heard from the neighbours
are to be entirely believed, Dan –
which I dare say they aren't. No. Not *entirely*."

[Oolala. Notheragainpolis!]

147

"It's simple, Eve. Get your basis in contentment –
then do your best to maximise the chances
of wonderful moments – right? – because, in the end,
that's how it all comes to us. Moments. Good or bad.
Indifferent too. Yes. Do I really have to repeat that?"

148

"Yes, thank you. Yes. That is certainly one
of your most delicate and valuable insights,
Adam. Which reminds me, Eadem –
there's something else I am going to have to tell you.
Now, first: promise me you *won't* get angry."

149

"No, dear, a fairly boring afternoon
all in all. Oh yes. One thing. I met
a talking snake which irritated me rather,
so I bit its head off." "What?" "What?" "Oh, God, darling!
For one thing, you're a much less *shy* girl than I took you for."

150
"Well, actually the rumour was
that the Devil himself – yes, the main one, you know? –
was likely to retire soon. Have you heard
anything like that where you come from? Is it,
would you say, even remotely plausible? No?"

151
"Oh, Dan, a lot of people overall
have [murdered] killed other people, you know, *Maestro.*
[Fortunately often for [religious reasons] the best of reasons.]
We try to keep them separate here, of course.
Paradise isn't really *quite* the right place
for wholesale regrets and recriminations, is it, dear? Still …
[We'll get it sorted out in the fullness of time, don't you worry!]

152
"Oh, after the next massive destruction,
others, with a bit of luck,
will no doubt start to build again, my darling.
But I'm afraid I couldn't care less.
No. I'm afraid, dear, I've just about had it."

[No reasonable person, I fear, could possibly agree with the author's own
suggestion, that it is Almighty God himself who is speaking here. There
are, after all, limits to everything – deference included.]

153
"A few [more] disasters, darling, and then
with a bit of luck
something at least slightly
better (or perhaps not).
What more, Adam, could we ever hope for?"

150

"And, you know, Eve, even if we somehow did
manage to produce an unaccountable genius –
or even, for that matter, merely a quite moderate one –
we almost certainly could not live long enough
to see this for ourselves. Isn't that right, darling?"

151

"No. Is it just me who's existing?
Is it me who's just existing? No.
What more did I ever want? Only this.
What else, my darling? What, for instance, would
an even better dying man be able to think of right now?"

152

No. It is not the sheer sunlight
which impresses me so much in this place
as the wispy smoke, the sense
of another day beginning
with all the right people at work somewhere hereabouts.

153

Oh, the uncapturable delight of those days!
That view, for instance, from the kitchen window!
Such a sheer gift! – I have kept it always with me.
Nothing but clouds of gratitude. No. But who else
could have been there, in real life, before you, before me?

154

"No, dear, this is Paradise.
Ask that just once more, dear,
and I'll start to think
there's something almost sinister
in your dear behaviour."

155

It's looks a fairly good morning, yes –
but more rain is forecast for later.
I don't know if we can quite trust it.
However, we might as well go. After all, darling,
we don't quite trust each other yet either, do we?

[What do you mean, *Mad Eye*?]

156

Yet how easily these days I can still recall
that ordinary pathway over the lawn
leading to her celestial flat:
past unknown curtained windows –
sometimes open; yes; sometimes closed.

157

Those ordinary calm streets beyond
the wall below her balcony window!
What palaces they must have led to!
(Or a mere quiet kink in the roadway
worth so much more than any celestial mansion.)

154

Look, dear! The same small path is still here
when I return –
what? – nearly forty years later.
(At least, erm, Eve, I'm pretty sure
it's still the same small path.)

155

Caught out by a sudden heavy noonday shower,
I take shelter beneath a roofed lane-entrance,
facing a tenement building in which, no doubt,
various people unknown to me are having a routine meal,
or a f★★★, or a shit, or, for instance, a helpful (accidental?) snooze.

[True, no doubt. The poet's eye, eh? Nothing like it, is there?]

156

More torrential rain!
What else is one to do?
Oh, well. If one absolutely
has to be getting old, one might as well
be stuck indoors all day too, I suppose.

157

"To be quite honest, my view is that I never made any really
important mistakes, Dao. (Well, none that I can
remember anyway!) For these days, you know, I spend
nearly all my time trying to prevent myself from obsessing over
ancient trivial ones – so trivial – much like yourself!"

158
"Well, it has to be about itself,
I suppose. I mean to say, darling,
there's nothing else here, is there?
Or, for that matter, there. So. What else
could the Ultimate be about, but all this?"

[I just love an imaginary world, and I don't care who knows it.
Of course, I do not intend to give my real name here.
I mean to say, I may not exist, but that doesn't mean I'm stupid!
(Does it?)]

159
For a few days or so
I have been able to treat this flat
as if it were my own. (Thank you, Eve.)
But how I wish I could do the same
with [my life] the universe in general!

160
And these bright new flowers in the kitchen too! Oh, how much
I wish I were really here! (As undeniably
here, for instance, as your curious, not-quite-the-same cats
seem to believe I am.) Not that I
doubt it deep down. (Do I?) No. (Deep down?) (NO!)

[No?]

161
Love eventually, my darling,
seeped out of some living beings
much as life itself must once
have seeped out of the leaves and stones —
(and who knows what might not come next?)

158
"Well, the great thing about my life
is that, erm – is that – errem –
oh, what was it now? – but
please don't interrupt me, darling –
I just *know* there was something there! Yes."

[Well, all right. I may perhaps be a non-existent God. But at least I'm
perfectly, um, open about it.]

159
"Well, Donke, we were at least left free
to write anything we wanted to –
even if this was mostly tired and worthless.
And how much worth would there have been in
whatever else we had bothered to do instead?"

160
The happiest moments of my life? –
But were many of them not merely –
well – a sort of sitting nonchalantly about
(with you, Eve, with you) in one otherwise
scarcely distinguished room after another?

161
(Oh, yes, darling – and a certain
amount was being done for me
there, elsewhere,
all the time too, I
have – (no offence) – to assume. Next!)

162
– and so we all somehow must crawl into real life
now through some ensanguined opening or other –
yes, Beatrice, even the most inspired of us; the most
given to make absurd but possible noises
about perfect, additional, thought-up and impossible other worlds;

[Yes. Himself, for instance. But one might think that a single Omniverse
would be enough for anybody!]

163
not from some other place where we were *before* –
before the circumstances that made us (as it happened) coalesced –
but from the uniquely real fine details that produced us;
from those complexities about which we learn so little –
(but who knows in advance how much we can possibly learn?) –

164
"You know, sometimes it crosses my mind,
O Socrates, that non-Existence
might be the greatest [sexual] conceptual perversion of all.
Oh, no – wait a minute. Wait a minute. No.
I've never really had that thought in my entire life, have I?"

165
"Yes. It's that comparative rarity –
a great work full of people
whom, Meremortal, it is impossible –
whom in fact it would be *a great mistake*
to take entirely seriously. All right?"

162

And yet, what is it all for, Adam?
For? For? For? For? Look! The Universe
is not some sort of tool, is it? Even so,
may I not rightly say that this indeed
is what all these incomparable days are for?

[But how, Mr Flucks, can one possibly say that the Universe is not 'for'
whatever, as it happens, happens to be happening in it? Eh?]

163

For I had such joy in this life
and this was in fact the life I had it in –
not in some merely imagined
conceptual rearrangement
but here in this swirling life itself, Lavinia –

("The entire Universe is a survival from a previous age." Though I admit
one is tempted to emend this to "from a future age" – or some such *jeu
d'esprit*. Sprite. Tripes. "The entire Universe is a threatened survival from
another age." Remove the last remark at least? Lavinia, of course, was the
name of Aeneas's wife.)

164

"Dear lass! Has no-one really ever told you this before?
But no. No, Vee: I dare say we are all at the slack mercy
of the odd, flukish, far-flung, inadequate languages
which our vain-vaulted predecessors have so so [un]kindly
hacked at and out or tuningly crashed and crushed for us."

165

The true poet (said the very wise head in the vat)
should not really care too much about the fact
that he cares so passionately about some things –
and these things, of course, O Oracle,
should, if possible, be all the right things, if any.

166

Even on the last morning of his long life –
yes, perhaps even within sight of reaching the full hundred –
still he will still find himself vaguely wondering
whether or not his real, his actual earthly existence
is soon about to start, and, if so, quite when.

167

I don't remember any of it, Adam.
Not a single detail, hardly.
Only that I was happy there.
Yes. More or less ridiculously happy.
Almost impossibly happy, I should say just now.

[But then, Vita, what ever does?]

168

"Oh, presumably they more or less all thought
they were discovering it for the first time.
And that millions of others, my darling,
had somehow managed to come and go earlier
without quite finding the same thing out for themselves."

169

But no, it seems
even our gross stupidities,
can so easily outlive ourselves.
(Much like the Universe itself
in fact, I dare say.)

166

"Somehow I would like to deny
that this one really is
a human being at all, Joe –
but the facts are all against me.
Or most of the facts at least."

167

He who knows for certain, Budd,
there can be no point to it all
does not sit about worrying
that there might be no point to it all –
for what would be the point of that?

[Needless to say, this has nothing whatsoever to do with what Vitus has
called 'the only true religion'.]

168

My parents – now not here – now nowhere –
but, oh, they're all dead now! –
whether they did it or
not, well or badly, or indeed
not at all. Still, Adam. Which of us cares really?

169

"For we do not quite grasp
the fact that we really die –
even those of us
who think we f***ing grasp it. Well,
I mean to say. Just look around you here!"

170
"In fact, I'm afraid I should have to claim, Thouth,
that, for most people for so much of the time,
the real world is evidently more
a series of rather clogged, unwelcome distractions
from the supposed reality of their favourite vast fantasies −

[Yes, yes, yes. An atrocious old bore, deep down. Of course, any fantasies
about reality, however unrealistic in themselves, are also, considered as
eruptions in the brain, a real part of the real world too. The amazing thing,
surely, is that such beings can live, breed and survive at all − even the ones
who suppose it can't really all be happening − whatever that might be taken
to mean!! −]

171
And suddenly the huge, not
unshattering thought occurred to the Master
just as he reached out to the summit of Heaven:
Here! Wait a minute!
This is all rubbish! Yes. All absolute balls!

172
Beyond this delightful attic window
a fenced public path runs by
at the edge of the wood
often unused for hours −
or perhaps even for the whole day.

173
Suddenly useless −
these keys to your old flat.
Where once, do you remember −
but what does all that matter now, Eve?
Assuming it ever mattered. (Which, of course, it did.)

[Which, of course, it certainly did.]

170

"And what a mean comfort it is, darling, when abroad,
to notice announcements of comparatively
unimportant local deaths
in the local newspapers – so! Look at this!
It seems, Eva, I am not the only transient here!"

[Is one ever the only one in transit anywhere?]

171

How can we prove to others that our faith
is chiefly a matter of love and justice? I know, Master!
Let's encourage the young, with their wonderful energy,
to enter hotels and attempt to shoot dead as many as possible
infidel (and therefore worthless) visitors more or less at random!

172

Occasionally, after hours of neglect,
two quite separate people
will appear on this neglected path—
moving, within the same few seconds,
not always in opposite directions.

173

Week after week
(while she visits some alluring parts of Asia)
that small clock of hers still ticks on in the bedroom –
a strangely loud, precise sound
[which once used to irritate me considerably.]
which used to irritate me ever so slightly sometimes.

174
From the plant there came
after so many years of silence
a single urgent cough – er, laugh.
And that was that!
Only a single fleeting laugh – er, no. Cough.

175
Yes. Buildings in every street –
and people at home in them all,
presumably, Ada(m).
Why shouldn't they be?
And not really somewhere else either!

[Ulm?]

176
Yes, Eve. I too have strolled down
a few of the most exquisite streets in Europe
strangely unrecognised.
(Not that I expected
to be recognised, of course.)

177
"Perhaps not having been killed –
or not yet, anyway, Beatrice –
for saying all this sort of stuff
is as much success as I
could reasonably have hoped for?"

178
Oh yes, sometimes merely
in cutting through an almost random side-street
one seems to get an unsought glimpse
of an entire contented life –
but what real life was ever so much like that?

174

And yet – just look how nonchalantly
your car tries to blend in
with all the other ones in this huge car park!
Why do so many people bother to drive these virtual
accidents – always off, off to the wrong bloody places!

175

From the planet there came
after so very many years of silence
a single fleeting laugh – er, no: a cough –
and that was that! Yes. (Well, no.)
Only a single urgent cough – er, yes: laugh.

[Rather mechanical, perhaps; but at least it makes a change from all the
farting.]

176

And all these rather charming
parts of the earth which I
could simply happen to stumble upon
(depending on where I was)
within the next few seconds!

177

"It's all right. Don't feel sorry for me.
The fact is, darling, I have already
walked in imagination down
some rather beautiful streets named after me –
all done with a suitable, glorious humility, I hope."

178

For the fact is, Gabriel –
if one is simply left free to get on with it –
then, ideally, one takes sublime advantage
of this fortunate state of affairs –
and, yes, one simply gets on with it.

179

So. We went out a walk, bought some cakes –
and unhurriedly returned. What does it matter, Eve,
if, to be honest, they really weren't all that good?
There was always the walk itself. Yes. Routinely there and back.
Anything more was a sheer surplus of humdrum joy.

[Earlier version? Enough to have lived / like that for five whole seconds! /
Anything else, Vie, / was sheer and lavish surplus / to our everyday joy.]

180

Bravely, I try to buy some fresh German cream cakes
using coins that had been lying in a drawer
far off in Glasgow, more or less forgotten,
uselessly foreign there, for nearly the last three years.
Incredible! This young woman here – accepts them instantly!

[Dreams in that district. So many cars too! And an artist lived somewhere
else on that street, did she not?]

181

Who is there, *Kind* – where in fact is the nearest person
who has walked through or down or even visited the street
in which these humdrum, undiscovered coins
were still being kept, say, at this time last week? But
we more or less never find out things like this, do we? No.

[I agree. And yet, if imaginative literature should not be about answering
questions like these, then I for one have no idea what it should better be
about.]

182

So. With a casual glance to the left
as I tourist-walk my way down this delicious small road
through a calm, plush, leafy German suburb
for the twentieth time or so – what? What on earth is *that*?
Yet another real street? How could I have missed it till now?

179

Yes. And as I next strolled down the central street of Heaven
with a little time on my hands, I happened to notice
a not uninteresting group of people [entities?] seated
in one of the major arcades. So I strolled gently towards them,
not entirely unconfident they would be [able] ready to recognise me.

180

The clunk of the letterbox again!
Only a single item today.
Dead for over fifteen years –
and yet the religious charities
are still appealing to her repeatedly proven good nature.

[In this case, I happen to know, a circular addressed to his mother at her
final known address.]

181

"Of course, we did not know then, during all those years,
that the very next occupier would commit suicide right there
in the rooms where we had been so happy. Or more or less blissfully
content at least. Did we, Eve? Assuming what we were told
is correct, of course. Which I have no great reason to doubt."

182

All right, Eve. Put your little skirt back on, since you have to,
and go and see who that is at your front door.
But if it isn't someone roughly as important
as God Himself – then treat him as I would have you treat
some unwanted past lover. Here. Take this [gun]gum with you.

183

I rush to the (at last!) ringing doorbell –
expecting it to be her (at last!) But no.
No. Instead, it is someone who purports to be an expert
in the installation of a complex new type of space-age
security window. He claims that some people even welcome him!

184

"That noise? Er – what does it matter really, Dan?
Some sort of wall may well have fallen down, I suppose.
A brief bout of misdirected high spirits, perhaps.
No. I don't think we ought to go and look at it, no.
No, Lord. I really would advise against it. Really."

185

"Oh, my, yes – but look! – what *utterly lovely*
big black wavy feathers those angels there have!
What exactly is the particular significance of that uniquely thrilling
     feature,
Beatrice? Hello? Beatrix? Bea? Beatrice? Beattie? Look:
I didn't make up the rules here, Beatrice, did I?"

[Well, yes, as a matter of fact, you did. Writers! Though I am certainly
mightily impressed by how often those who comment on Dante and such-
like (sacred scriptures, etc.) talk as if the writer really had witnessed or
visited the fantastic scenes he describes.]

186

"Oh, as far as I can make out, Adam – er, Franz – er, Eighth Dan –
at least 96% of them were absolute halfwits –
and this may well be a charitable understatement.
Oh, yes. I could have made them much better, of course.
But that would hardly have been quite fair to them, would it?"

183

Oh, don't worry about it, darling, she shouted
as I went flying head-first out of the nearest window –
it isn't what it seems! (But then, it hardly ever is, is it?)
And don't worry about *him* either.
He knows *exactly* what he's doing [wrong].

184

"No. It can't possibly be *His* fault. How could it be?"
"Natheless, don't all our faults, Beatrice,
have to come from God (ye Pantocrator!) anyway –
if ultimately he controlleth everything? I mean, hen, how else – "
"But that's not the point, Dan! Oh – and I genuinely thought you
loved me!"

185

"Oh, yes, a sublime concert! How wonderful it was
to watch her playing that noble instrument –
while her gorgeous wings fluttered, heavenly music
poured in diapason out of her various apertures
and – er – that *was* Sir Jock Schubert himself conducting, was it
not?"

[It was. Alas, Big Jim Mozart had to be abroad at the time.]

[*Hen* is a very common Chinese intensive, by the way.]

186

"Yet hearken well, Dante. The physical world
is and *can only be* an analogy
for the 'impossible' and the 'incoherent' –
which itself, Dan, can only be expressed
allegorically by the physical. [Just so.
Now please F★★★ OFF, you highly disagreeable deviant!]"

187
"Oh, yes – take risks in thought! Why else bother?
But not in life – which is always a risk anyway.
Breathing is itself hazardous enough, I find.
And I'm not just saying this, believe me, Dante,
because I'm immured for all eternity in a Great Wall of shit."

[One of my guardian angels is absolutely sure that this is Genghis Khan
speaking here. (A by no means ridiculous suggestion, let me add, however
[ridiculously] optimistically.) Certainly some denizen of Hell.]

188
While the great man was having a particularly difficult shit,
in a sudden epiphany, he felt he realised
what would be the absolute best for the country he loved.
"But I dare say I may be mistaken even here too,"
he nobly thought – as slowly he keeled over onto his face.

[Dead, I assume, Lord?]

189
"If I had only been
even a tiny bit taller, Dan,
I quite possibly wouldn't have had a single *major*
problem to deal with in my entire life! But no. No.
That's what comes of simply having the wrong f***ing parents!"

[Oh, if only different people had been slightly *different* different people!
That could surely have made a quite crucial difference!]

187
"But does it even exist? Can we be sure of that?"
"Well, yes. Yes; of course it does."
"What? Excuse me. Does *what* even exist?"
"Go away, darling! This has absolutely *nothing*
to do with you. Right, Lord. What the f★★★ were we talking about?"

188
Oh, I may be wrong here, darling.
Yes. I may be quite wrong here.
Of course, I was somewhere else
for at least most of the time.
But then again, who wasn't?

[A fairly unusual form of political epitaph, certainly.]

189
If Truth lay dulled on this hallway table
between a large, heavy torch and the box
you brought that pizza here in with you last night –
then I might well try to decorate it
with these two ribbon-rays that once tied up – er – what?

[Obviously included here, Doctor, for some obscurely profound personal
reason which is nowadays scarcely recoverable.]

190
And all those [bedroom] doors
being walked so forcefully through right now!
Or else, maybe, just standing there –
you know – like that one – presumably
either open or shut. Yes?

191
and as much an item in the universe too
as, say, was Mr J★★★★ C★★★★★ –
to pluck out yet one more name
from the ever-remoter past –
that tiny black thing scuttling over your carpet there –

192
Oh, you're beautiful! –
thank you so much for existing –
or whatever it is you're doing –
and as for what *I* am doing – well –
do you have a favoured opinion yourself?

193
"Look, darling, you are not something
which was somehow already there –
and which your genes then, as it were, came along
and happened to [fastened onto?] – no, I am not resorting
to personal abuse again – no! Certainly not! What?"

190

Look there! Nearly hidden by a voluminous tree,
a second-floor window in the very next street –
which I had never really noticed before!
That's a nice big terrestrial globe up there, is it not?
And a bust of someone? (No doubt a towering genius!)

[Shouldn't this have been placed opposite 182? Not for the first time it
occurs to me that the ordering hereabouts has gone badly wrong. But perhaps
that makes it all the more appropriate as regards life, the universe etc. etc.]

191

By the time he heard the knocking
and went to answer the door
there was again no-one there!
(Not that he greatly worried.
(In fact, he scarcely even noticed.))

192

"As far as I can remember,
he even claimed to exist!"
"What, Darling?
The arrogance of the man!
(If man indeed he was!)"

193

In fact, my angel, love
is one more of the tools which developed in the game.
Tools, yes. A further move. Oh, a real thing, of course;
and, of course, fairly negligent-wondrous – but hardly
something that dropped down into here from a non-existent beyond.

["Negligent-wondrous"? What's this? You too can sound like Shake-
speare? (Though not terribly like him.)]

194
"How could all this conceivably have been the wrong life, Eve?
How could it have been? Or is this the wrong Universe?
But how could it have been that either? Was I then perhaps
the wrong person? Yes? Compared to what not-here person?
All that exists to be thought of as the wrong Existence!"

[Indeed. If this is the wrong Everything, no wonder we can't ever quite
feel at home in it! Actually, for a long time, once the juvenile sense of
novelty wore off, I used to feel as if I weren't quite leading my own life.
But lately, if anything I at times seem to have lost most even of that residual
degree of belongingness – if you or your [non-surviving] twin know what
I mean, dear.]

195
But if the All-Powerful
doesn't really want it –
then how could it happen at all, Eve?
(I know, I know. Not terribly original.
But just answer the question, will you?)

196
"You know, there is something going on here," –
said Almighty God with a frown –
"which, truly, I am rather afraid
I can't even begin to understand. Right!
Get my brother on the new phone, will you, Gabrielli?"

197
"Er. Hello?
This new Universe, Mate?
What are we supposed to do with it?
Where are we supposed to put it? Eh? What? Well now –
there's really no need for that sort of language, Matey."

194

"Just hand me over that other universe instead —
will you, Beatrice, m' dear? Thank you. That should do it.
I much prefer it to this somewhat duller one here,
don't you? We'll scrub it. This one here, I think.
It probably has too many gases, insects and languages."

Which reminds me. I should perhaps have mentioned earlier — though it
hardly matters much now (what does? (and what is 'earlier' anyway?)) —
that the range of meanings given for 'Dan' in my dear old friend Owbank's
much-thumbed and very ancient Chinese lexicon include: Dawn,
morning, an egg, a pill, simple (as opposed to *complex*), but, odd (as
opposed to *even*), tasteless or insipid, red, and a female impersonator. So.
There's the novel half-written already. (Not to mention the *Autobiography*.)

195

Oh, I have now reached the stage, I fear, Adam [Dad?],
when the whole Universe merely seems
to be, as it were, a sort of brilliant
obsolete image of itself — and now
packed so full of absolutely the wrong people! —

196

"Perhaps suddenly it has taken off
from this drab flat surface, Raphael,
for an almost equal surface
even now erotically [exotically?] waiting
in its own drab golden elsewhere?"

197

"Kept awake once more
by a recurrence of an annoying earache
I quietly switched on the bedside lamp —
and discovered to my surprise, Eve, that
there were at least three people in the room."

198
"Oh, if only I could have come back
as someone else entirely, Adam,
I suspect that I (or
that other person) might have been
a whole lot happier then. No?"

199
"How true that is, And.
Such very similar names!
And yet, who can say
quite how many more people
might really be involved here?"

['And' is obviously a name here. (Though surely not an abbreviation of
'Andrea'?)]

200
"No. No, I decided I didn't really want
to be back in, you know, that earlier Universe –
you know, where the thought of – you know –
with the woman you love, for that matter –
could even be put into words. Yes. You know? No?"

201
Yes. So. Here we sit, darling. You and I. –
(An absolute riot of clever bacteria inside and out.) –
Wondering, among much else, what Love is.
Wondering what perhaps is going to happen tomorrow.
While elsewhere the maniacs of certainty fart on about eternity.

[One way of putting it, I suppose.]

198
"Well, none of them
are me [– i.e. Reality –],
are they, Adam?
So in some sense, they must
only be pretending – no?"

199
"No. I still can't work out
quite how many voices
are supposed to be speaking here.
[Is that] Beatrice? I keep hearing things.
Or at least, I think I keep hearing things."

[Why not?]

200
"But what the Hell would you know about it, Adn?
And how many other human beings, tell me, for that matter,
have passed right through, in and out of life,
forever supposing themselves to be the fathers of children
who were in fact the furtive crudities of other people?"

[Yes. And so many must expire with so many of their ([even] long[est]-
standing) delusions still more or less intact and undamaged.]

201
"Oh, I can assure you, Beatrix,
I have rarely if ever felt any great desire
to attempt to copulate with – er – er –
but why exactly are we talking about this
anyway? I wished to discuss Eternity."

202

"Oh God no, we're not allowed
to talk about that in here. And, besides,
very few of us would ever want to.
Though we must get at least an occasional weird intruder
pretty much like anywhere else does, I suppose."

203

"Yes, of course it is ridiculous
to worship women, Danna — as if
they too were not another form of the human.
On the other hand,
at least women *are really there*, are they not?"

204

Well, am I supposed to be able to see her
or not, I wondered.
It's not so easy to know.
I'm absolutely certain she's there. Yes.
I'm absolutely certain that's her shimmering over there.

205

"And what's that wonderful big billowing entity
over there, Beatrice?" "That? Oh, I've no idea."
"No? You've really no idea what it is, darling?"
"Yes. No. I've really no idea. Where? Anyway —
if it's here, its almost certainly insubstantial too."

[By what if any conceivable method, in other words, is the insubstantial to
be located and identified? (Particularly by something [else?] which is itself
insubstantial? Though, curiously enough, the idea that, as it were, both
entities — the immaterial 'perceiver' and the immaterial 'perceived' — are
both devoid of substance and sensory apparatus alike has the air of lessening
the difficulty rather than impounding it. (At least the impossibles here are
perfectly matched!))]

202
"For life after life
goes on even so
in room after room after
room – while we – erm – while – erm – but tell me:
just what exactly *are* we doing here, Beatrice?"

203
Well. what sort of answer can anyone
ever give to that?
To how large a question, O Seventh Dan –
wake up! – can any single neat answer
ever contrive to be adequate? Yes? I'm waiting.

204
"Oh, she would have been
perfect for me! Totally
perfect for me! Oh,
it's a sublime tragedy
I haven't yet met her here!"

205
"No, no, no – Dan! No.
It's blasphemy even
to listen to such crap! Absolutely not!
Look. There's a perfectly simple reason why
none of them have any actual physical details as such!"

[Surely that much at least is simple enough, Amad? All real existence, in the
end – and usually in the beginning too! – is a matter of *physical* existence.
(Nothing can exist without a physical substrate, be it never so ethereal.)]

206
"But perhaps no religious idea
could ever be as brilliant
and at the same time as ridiculous
as the concept of reincarnation, could it, my dear Dan?
(Um. That's always assuming you *are* Dante, of course.)"

207
"However, no longer delay! Have you by any chance
come to take me away, my dear good biped,
to a place where I'll be happier than I am here?
Because, my darling, if you have – erm –
there's [at least] one important thing I'll have to tell you first."

208
"Indeed, yes! To come back (from where?)
as someone so radically different
while both remaining the same different person! –
yes! that's the only right way to do it, Adam!
(Or whoever, darling, it is you really are.)"

209
"You know, to be quite honest, Beatrice,
I admit I'm having a certain amount of difficulty
in recognising all these insubstantial essences
which are sort of, as it were, unfloating about
in this non-specific place. Hello? Hello?"

210
"Well, these present (let us hope, only passing) conditions
are hardly all that conducive, are they, Dien,
to genuine, long-lasting reform? Look. Here.
Just hold this ****ing awkward halo
for me for a moment, will you, dear? Good. Thanks."

206

"Distant? Distant? Well, of course I look
distant. Be reasonable! How else
is an imaginary being supposed to look?
These personal-appearance decisions
don't just make *themselves*, you know."

207

"Oh, yes, Dantex – one *appears* to die, to disintegrate –
nonetheless, what *really* happens is that, somehow,
an insubstantial element lurking somehow in
or to or from some unfathomable elsewhere – featureless,
but somehow not to be confused with nowhere – er – oh, ★★★★! –

208

I heard the back door open and shut
and I knew it must be you.
A couple of polite footsteps.
Then a [strange] voice tentatively
calling out: "Hello? Anyone there?"

209

How much I envied her, for all that,
her sweet nature, her smile –
and the fact that almost to the end
she could always remove either head so easily
whenever she especially wanted to.

210

"Oh, the truth is, dear Penelope, I never had
a single serious clue – did I? –
in all my bloody life! (And yet, to know
that they were right there beside me could at times
be such an immortal comfort, I gladly admit.)"

211
And how much joy is there in this street too? (Guess?)
Or in the next (rather shorter) one? – (Or grief?)
Fairly content at the moment, thanks – pretty much as usual –
and also, darling, I'll have to phone you later
to let you know you've left your Paisley scarf behind –

212
"Just imagine! Year after year after year –
to have a sort of useless sound ringing
endlessly in either (or both) of one's ears.
I could never have stood it myself, Eve.
No wonder he created such a distracting universe."

[Certainly an improvement on the one that used to be in place here!
("Him, Eve? I don't know. He has the sort of / delusional exaltation one
associates / either with ingrained religious obsession / or advanced syphilis
– or in / some cases, of course, both at once.")]

213
Oh! I thought I had thrown this music out
years ago, darling –
but I haven't!
And, of course, it's not quite
what I'm looking for right now.

214
"So. I thought to myself:
Well, I won't be here for long.
I'll leave the worst of the tasks
for the next occupier to deal with.
Shows how much I knew, Dan, eh? Frnarf."

[I doubt whether the final word there really is either a name or the
profoundest secret of the Universe. Of course, I may be wrong.]

211

"So, my unique darling.
I have come through another year –
with your help. Though God
knows quite why. Which does rather remind me.
Why do you still have ordinary days here?"

212

"Frankly, Adam, I doubt
whether it was all that important a mistake
really. For who else, darling,
can or does this universe belong to
any more than it can or does to us?"

["Yes! Great! / I have finally broken through / into non-Existence! All you
others / everywhere round about me! / Hello? Hello! Hello?"]

213

"Oh, beyond a certain point,
Eve, the more one learns about
(and understands) the past –
surely the more
utterly bloody unbearable it becomes? No?"

214

"What? Not easily forgotten?
What more can you have hoped for?
How could it have been otherwise, Beatrice?
What else is anyone ever doing here
but farting [bravely] while the Universe shudders all round – "

["But God is *allowed* / to be wrong about nearly everything," / said a
passing Arch Wave. / "That is half the point / of being God in the first
place."]

215

"Surely I'll never use these keys again?
So why do bother to I keep them?
Sheer laziness, I suppose.
Besides which – how much of anything,
my delightful girl, does anyone ever use again?"

216

The last time I listened to this not very special music
it was in a small sunlit kitchen near a park
where we – but what does it matter? what, you might ask,
does it all matter? Yes. Then say what matters more
than a morning's subdued routine gently swaying in bliss.

217

Evidently and innocently misunderstanding
what it was I'd been complaining about,
she put her cup down, leant nimbly over,
stuck her little tongue into my ear
and breathed out a magic word several times.

218

Most of us, I suppose, would die pretty happy
if we could only hear, even once,
the caring voice of the Universe saying to us directly:
"Hello, love. I think you're a really nice person. Yes, really.
No. I'm not just saying that. Believe me. Yes. *Really* nice."

["Yes. But *please* don't ask me what the other half is, sweetheart."]

215
Yea, hand the poor depressed man some apple juice quickly –
thick and gold as a helpful Goddess's primary exudation –
and, after that, perhaps
hand me – er, *him* – this morning's latest lying newspaper
for a quick and probably contemptuous perusal before –

216
And if I had not
wakened up again
(and again, Eve, and again, Genevieve) –
in whichever invariably modest room
I happened to find myself? –

217
God, God! What a lad I am!
Do all these other people really deserve
to be sharing the planet with me?
[Do I really not have one to myself?]
And yet, each morning, I receive precisely
no Thank You letters whatsoever!

218
Only when I turned fifty-six,
did (I think) I finally realise
that I was not in fact from Outer Space!
(I can still hardly believe, Mrs Ordobonis-Quadriofax,
it took me quite so long to notice this!)

[Well, yes. But aren't we all, in a rather obvious sense, from Outer Space
anyway?]

219

You know, I don't really too much like the fact
that it's seventeen minutes past three in a winter morning.
No. If the Universe were to stop dead right now –
(assuming it hasn't done so already, Odysseus) –
you certainly wouldn't hear me for one complain!

220

I waken up rather surprisingly refreshed
from a dream in which I more than once slapped
my present landlord's large fat face [with a fish].
Though, I dare say, on the whole undeservedly –
I feel I perhaps (as a gross coward) ought to add.

221

As I said to my soon-to-be-ex-wife in bed only last night:
"This whole situation in Colombia –
er, sorry, darling, in Venezuela –
is getting rather worrying these days, isn't it,
darling? Darling? Darling? Darling – are you *really* asleep?"

222

You know, at the last Endless Universal Dream Olympics
I must say I thought my final mark was far too low –
(but who can the strangely inadequate judges be?)
All the same, I intend to lodge a strong appeal anyway –
[where? or perhaps merely to dream it?]
whatever in fact it was I must have been doing instead.

223

Morning after morning –
on the shelf in the bathroom
while I shave myself yet again –
a tiny tired heap of old bones
which (I think) almost never move.

219
The man in the next
hospital bed told me that he
had lived just round the corner from this
very building all his life – though his son
was in fact at present working in [New Zealand] Nepal.

220
"Oh, I went to hear a lecture
called *What Is Man Good For?* –
but, alas, it had been cancelled.
So, rather at a loose end, my Beatrice,
I went off to see a challenging Belgian sex-film instead."

221
"You have done more or less
nothing for me, my darling creature;
but nonetheless I still sort of forgive you.
if you had done even a little more
I'd possibly have missed such a unique storm of beauty."

222
"Right, my dear, saintly Friend.
This is the deal in a nutshell.
Either I'll play with your emotions
or I'll completely ignore you. All right?
So. Which would you prefer?"

223
"Well, Everrem, what image
is there anywhere
which is not in fact just sitting around
waiting to become obsolete –
eh? And why has she got three legs?"

224
But why do I keep reconstituting
so many acute unwanted moments
of long-past embarrassment?
It's not as if they were even
of any continuing importance, is it, Lord?

225
"I don't know – er – Eve.
I really don't know. No, really.
I dare say it must just all have happened
while I was not quite working women out.
You know? And [doing] a few other, no doubt less vital things."

226
"Sometimes when I try to think
just quite how many skeletons
have walked about the earth so far – and indeed
are walking about right now, Danthes – for some no doubt
[apparently] urgent reason or other – "

227
"Oh, you know, dear – a gradual loss of function
all the time – (what little can even I still do?) –
with occasional massive depreciations;
while the brain of brains tries to cling on for dear life
(at least, I assume it's still clinging on, my very dear
        whatever-your-name-is) – "

228
"Shit! I'm dead, Ulysses!
No – wait a minute. Wait a minute.
How can I be dead? Hmm.
(Well, for that matter –
how could I have been *alive*?)"

224

There was no-one else in the house but us.
Eagerly, Joseph, I pulled her neat little skirt up
and, even more eagerly, her neat little knickers down.
Then, to be quite honest, by now more than a little
suspicious, I asked: "Hello! What on earth is that?"

225

How bewitchingly, Vitalia, the autumn leaves are falling
by the bench in the lane here beside the dappling stream.
Much as, I suppose, throughout the large nearby city
the underwear of so many delightful girls must be delicately –
but, no! No. Just keep your stupid eyes on the delicate stream.

226

While, down in that neat low private garden
near where the stream runs past
the long calm wall at the back of the town cemetery,
stands a little statue of an elegant, classical goddess
which I must admit I have often rather felt like groping [at least].

[Stockdorf? – if I remember rightly. Yes. Yes.]

227

"I was dreaming about your sexual equipment", she added.
I could tell immediately from her mere tone of voice
that to show any interest in this
would be a huge mistake. On the other hand, my darling,
how I could convincingly *not* betray an interest in it?

228

"But how long it takes us to learn
what proper behaviour is!
Listen. Yesterday I chanced to meet
a once besotted old girlfriend. You wouldn't *believe*
what she said to me, Eve! Go on! Just try to guess."

229
"So. Who was it died up there
above our heads yesterday morning?
It wasn't me. (Was it?)
Or was it perhaps you? No. Excuse me,
Eve. No. That was a stupid question, I admit."

230
"What? Talk about
expecting too much!
You've gone too far
there this time, darling. Yes.
But wait. What's this? Should I really be dying too?"

231
"Oh God, Adam, I've only just
realised: Listen. Surely my own *mother*
must have died in this very bed!"
"But you don't have a mother, Eve. Do you?"
"Um. Darling, I know I should *probably* have told you this before …"

232
"Yes, Menelaus. On my wedding night
I used a valuable torch
left to me by my experimental father
to help me search for one or two fairly vital things
somewhere about us in the darkened bedroom."

233
Actually, I dreamt I was sprawled out on the bed –
pretty much the opposite way round
to how I found myself lying when I woke up!
(Too odd. And yet, *everything else*
was, in effect, exactly as it had seemed to be.)

229
"Oh, but I have long since grown tired
of all these half-witted idiots, darling – yes –
and I dare say most of these half-witted idiots
are pretty much tired of me too. Please. Is there any chance,
do you think, that you could take me away from here now?"

230
"Good God, darling! You know –
that thought never really got through to me
until I was nearly, what,
fifty-nine years old! How astonishing!"
"But surely you died when you were fifty-five, Dan. No?"

231
"Well, darling, I thought! –
this must undoubtedly be
the very same bed! –
surely it was old enough? –
yes – look! there's that strange rough edge – "

232
oh, great, darling! – look!
another eye here in bed right beside us!
eh? please –
you are scaring my children! –
(and my children are, as usual, absolutely terrifying me!)

233
That wonderful but chilling atlas
of close-up photographs
of different parts of the moon
must still be somewhere in that pile of books,
I think, just beyond our rumpled bed.

234
And in the morning, oh
God, yes – it's still there! Yes! It's
still there, Eve! Thank
God for that at least! Yes. For a moment,
I was afraid I might have lost it!

235
Does God exist?
Well, for that matter,
do my hands exist?
Yes. I think they must.
Look! Count them! One ... Two ... Three ...

236
"Yes, there was a good chance
that I might have indeed married her,
Eve – had she not
at just the wrong moment
become pregnant by another man."

237
Six weeks later,
when I was back in her flat,
the book was still lying there
on top of the hall-table
where I had slammed it down on leaving.

238
I am so pleased to be able
to help out in this difficult political situation
she said – deftly
kneeling down on the rug and
unfastening her narrow golden belt.

234

"Perhaps, in some sense, Eva,
we are all more or less merely pissing
right over the sharp edge of the known Universe?"
"Oh, please don't talk crudely like that, darling. No.
I'm afraid it isn't even *remotely* attractive."

235

"Oh, yes, darling, I dare say we shall meet –
shall doubtless live out our great loves,
and die and disappear in our slightly ridiculous turn too –
and all these various strange large rocks will continue
to gyrate about through space, yes, more or less as before."

236

"Oh, this locally celebrated love between men
and – er – women is ridiculous enough, as God well knows –
but, I mean to say, those seventeen even sillier sorts!
Indeed, how variously and easily" – (said the little Angel, pouting
with its gorgeous buttocks) – "may people be made gross fools of!"

237

"We seem to have nothing in common, my darling Eve –
except perhaps for the certainly not uninteresting fact
that roughly every few days or so I experience a strong desire
to copulate with you non-stop for a couple of hours at least.
So. What do you think? Can that be *the real thing*?"

238

When at last, with some disgraceful difficulty,
we helped each other back up off the kitchen floor again –
(a genuine miracle, Heav, if the word has any meaning!) –
the shamefully abandoned food nearby
was still uneventfully (and, it seemed, successfully) maturing.

[Oh, well. At least something was behaving in a mature way.]

239

"I'm afraid, Dange, that when I first heard her scream:
'Do whatever you like with me, you sick, sad beast!' —
my mind instantly started to work out
as exactly as it could, the fullest and foulest details
of the filthiest thing I could ever hope to get away with here."

[Here is, I assume, *Hell*. (Or some sort of hell at least.)]

240

"That sort of thing still excites you, does it, Daniel?
Hmm. Well, of course, given that these ones are
essentially spiritual beings — the wonder is, surely,
that they have *anything* in the way of the typical
effect of what is normally rooted in, you know, physical charms."

241

"The fact is, Beatrice, these days, in the mornings,
I seem to get much or most of my happiness merely
out of defecating successfully. Hmm. Yes. I remember
it used to come from listening to the early Beethoven
Violin and Piano Sonatas. Yes. Dear me. Not *quite* the same, is it?"

[You know, I have always rather tended to the belief that Bach at his best
must surely resemble a rather interesting lesson in mathematics, given
simultaneously by several appallingly beautiful teachers at least one of
whom is shatteringly nude? Or am I wrong here?]

239

"For which true, red-blooded male can there be, my Beatrix,
who has never at least once passionately wished to see – yes! –
say, George Eliot, her noble face no doubt contorted by pleasure,
as she jiggles her huge aristocratic jugs right in front of him
as a generous gift to himself – probably somewhere in Hampstead?"

['George Eliot' is, of course, a man's name. Not to be confused with 'T.S.
Eliot' – the well-known public-house and stage entertainer. 'Hampstead' is
evidently some sort of place-name. Head stamp. Hated maps. Death maps.
Death spam. Made paths. Of course there must be others.]

240

But what strange things must happen throughout this huge building!
First, she sat in her dull office, soberly discussing with me
a trip to Venice. And then, within ten minutes,
there I was, Deant, absurdly whacking away at her
in the only sheltered corner we could reach in time.

[I'm not proud of it. Oh, all right – I *am* proud of it!]

241

"Had I ever thought, she then asked me,
that women might be superior to men?
Lord, I did not need to reply.
No. We simply carried on
as if the point had tacitly been agreed."

[Might this possibly have something to do, Xanthe, with the *Policyan*
Form?]

242
Listen to those bloody sexual deviants
laughing next door, Eve,
in the wrong language entirely!
and the phone beside the bed
was never once proven necessary!

243
Oh God, no! – that hellish hint of involuntary
disappointment which edged into her voice –
when she realised the person phoning her
was only myself – (*me*!) – and not (presumably) the expected
new and far more wonderful personal interest in her life.

["Let us all just pretend," said the Recording Angel, "that none of this ever
happened."]

244
"So. Here was me, Lord, thinking, getting closer
to genuinely profound thoughts
than has ever been done before –
and now you tell me I have to
get up and go, just like that? Can that possibly be right?"

245
"Why? Because I pointed out that we urinate
and so forth every day – that sexual acts
produced us, yea, even the most austere of us –
that we stop moving, rot away, and cease to exist
in a rather self-evident manner. Yes. That, I suppose, is why."

242

"Frankly, Dante, I find your attitude utterly distasteful. Yes.
Hurtful. Unhelpful. Shockingly lacking in respect. In fact,
it *staggers* me. I feel wounded by it. Unintelligibly insufficient.
So inadequate. Still. Let's say no more about it, shall we?
Oh no, wait a moment. There was something else. Let me see.
        What was it now?"

243

Listen to me, Son. One of the main problems is
that men tend to assume very easily
they somehow just are more central than women are –
and women usually know, very easily, from the inside, that, actually,
to say the least, they aren't. Can't you grasp even that?

[So many commas! But sometimes it can be *such* a tactical advantage to be
under-estimated, can't it?]

244

"Yet how wonderful it is, Eve,
to sit here in a small quiet room together
talking about other uncapturable lives!
If only all these flimsy walls would stop
vibrating and collapsing all about me! (Sorry! About *us!*)"

245

"Oh, God, yes, Eve – I've been having a superb
succession of small, deep thoughts for at least
the last decade or so, I should say. Certainly I ought
to have written some of them down, I know. Yes.
I've no-one to blame for it but, erm – well, but myself, I suppose."

246
"Well, like very many fairly profound thinkers, Dan,
I – er – well, to be quite honest about it,
I died a long time ago
and I never really did have all that much
of a clue about anything genuinely important. Hmm. Sorry."

[Commendable honesty, at least. Presumably not an inhabitant of *Paradise*
speaking?]

247
"And in fact, to be quite honest, I very much doubt
whether there are any real deep deliberated mysteries
at all in our known Universe, if I may call it that –
except of course for the ones,
which we ourselves create. Know what I mean, dear?"

248
"And then, after all the possibilities
have indeed been realised –
what then? What next?
(Annihilation anyway, Eve,
I do these days rather tend to presume.)

249
"Yes. I believe I may well
have outlived my time by now – but then,
since it never quite seemed real to me,
I can't help but think we emerge
more or less equal from this. Don't you agree?"

250
No. My dear Adam or Eve, quite possibly no-one –
(*and by all means name here any real person, if you can*) –
is actually living anywhere
the sort of life you fear
that you, uniquely, might perpetually be missing –

246
"And then, as soon as I achieve
one glancing aspect of the impossible –
off I go chasing a completely different one!
Yes. It's a full-time job this, darling, this
pursuit of the life that lies beyond real life!"

[Om?]

247
"Oh, well. Life is basically a test – and has to be –
which we all must eventually fail. Something like that.
Except, I dare say, Duns, that it isn't really,
and that we don't – not really. Yes. Yes. Yes,
I think that gets quite a good part of it fairly well."

248
Beyond the causes – well –
further causes, no doubt.
Or beyond the ultimate edge –
Oh no! Surely not a further ultimate edge?
(A choice of utterly final drops, I presume?)

249
"Well, yes, Eve – somebody
made rather a hash of my life
certainly – and I only hope (whatever
circumstances might suggest to the
contrary) that it wasn't *really* me."

250 [*An Epitaph?*]
Bury me beneath a stone
inscribed with the wrong name and date
[as I dare say it so often is!]
and, underneath that, write
the great mystical-symbolic truth:
You know, I still feel somewhat out of place here.

251

And do even I dare to say that even Existence –
and, indeed, for that matter, non-Existence –
are both very often greatly over-rated, Even?
(Necessarily so at least at times, perhaps,
by anything with a suitably advanced brain?)

["The Universe, Chan, is nothing but a large door between different
nowheres. Look how the crowds flee through in [joy or] terror either one
way or the other!" (*Dogem.*)]

252

But what if she were to say:
"All right then. Go!
Just go!" What would I do?
Hmm. Just go, I suppose.
Can it really still be that easy?

253

"Hmm. A pleasant, unlooked-for
ambiguity! Perhaps I had better
stop there," said the Lord.
(Though, personally, Eve, I
was not yet even aware he had started!)

254

"Darling, I saw how the sentence
was going to end – didn't like the look of it –
and so decided not even to start it.
Isn't that enough
real freedom of movement for any thinker here?"

251

Or perhaps just give him
the routine but magnificently accurate epitaph:
I never really knew
very much about nearly anything, did I? –
and now I'm stone dead anyway. *Alas.*

[Or, rather: *not even that.*
(i.e. not even dead. After all, people have died by now in their almost
incomputable millions – but not even one of them exists onwards in some
sort of state of *being dead*. For there is no being of them left to be anything,
in any state of actual personal being. I could say more but I dare say I, er –
hic, etc.) I'll be completely silent from now on.]

252

Look, Beatrice! Another gorgeous evening
is subsiding slowly into
the trees behind the tedious little cemetery nearby.
I dare say most of them
must have been parents too. No?

253

My life has pretty much
been destroyed, Doctor,
by the creative impulse.
Still. I don't remember being
offered any choice here.

254

Ah, God, yes! – how wonderful
life was, before
one had developed any clear,
realistic idea, dear, of what
so many other people would be like!

255
Listening to a lawyer opposite me
receive a very indiscreet phone-call
while I was on the train –
I once again congratulated myself, Neve,
that I was, to an important extent, quite invisible.

256
Such interesting snippets of conversation
one hears on the train these days
(thanks to the mobile phone) –
"Yes! You should have seen the ones
I had to leave out, darling!"

257
"Oh God, Eve – I'm so sorry
if this isn't very flattering –
but – erm – oh never mind.
No. Just forget it. No.
I said: Just *forget* it! *All right?*"

258
"Now. How the hell can I ever
get out of this," thought God – "with my
reputation intact? Hmm. I know! I know – I'll just
annihilate this entire universe and
replace it with an even better one! Brilliant. TUNC!"

[How then can it matter much what is written above the Doors and in
what language(s)?]

255
"What? Who did you say was there?
Who? *Who*? Are you quite serious?
Hmm.
Well, I think, in that case, Master,
I'd really rather go somewhere else – "

256
O, all ye (even if non-existent) Gods,
please please please please –
please don't let *any*
of our ridiculous old love-letters
survive in any way whatsoever anywhere!

257
Such interesting snippets of conversation
one hears in passing these days
(thanks to the mobile phone) –
"Save us from what exactly?
What is there to be saved from?"

[I don't know. Death and annihilation, possibly? (Just a guess.)]

258
Such interesting snippets of conversation
one hears from passing phone-users these days –
"Oh, I suppose most people
are never quite convinced
by their own fatal illnesses, darling."

259
"Truly, a wonderful race," said Veild.
"Yes, indeed. A truly wonderful race.
Never, for instance, shall I forget the heroism
[with which they all so adamantly refused to accept the truth]
with which they all so adamantly refused to deny the truth
of what was absolutely staring them forever in the face."

[The reality of death and subsequent total personal disappearance, I
suppose. What else? Sorry if I'm repeating myself. (Always assuming, of
course, subject to correction, (whether resisted or not), that that's who I
am and that that's what I'm actually doing.) (*Vide* remarks on ultimate
wisdom elsewhere.) Vilde?]

260
"For, Adam, who among us does not wish to be told
that deep down *the whole thing* cares for you and your loved ones –
and that *somehow* in the end absolutely everything
is going to be all right – so don't you worry about it?
How difficult is this to understand or sympathise with?"

[We do indeed.]

261
No! At first she simply would not accept
that so great a man could now really be dead.
She stayed there, clinging to the body, for a full couple of days.
Until, it seems, the truth finally dawned on her
and she went off for a sleep and, a little later, breakfast.

259
"Oh yes, in my youth I wished so long and deep
for the blissful peace of eternal death, my beloved Eve.
But now, decades later – ("But *I* do, of course!") –
when death is appreciably closer to me every day,
I – er – well, dear, in fact, who particularly cares?"

260
Even so, the ground fact is –
that dreadful things
really can happen, my darling;
and that we certainly
do die anyway.

[Hmm. Listen, Master – er, Mister. However, and however true, this is
hardly a message of much use or help or comfort to those of us, for
instance, who are entrusted with the somewhat necessary task of bringing
up a family, is it? (Fortunately, there are many other things we can say –
even the most depressing of us – which turn out to be well worth saying, if
only we can somehow get hold of them.) To deny the truth is no doubt a
terrible thing – but I trust we may be allowed from time to time to ignore
it? Or, at the very least, to neglect one part of it in favour of another? And
even if the author doesn't particularly agree with this, we know that that
hardly really matters, don't we?]

261
But, in the end, he died without realising it –
pretty much as he had lived.
On the other hand, what else could he do –
or should he have done? It's not as if you *have* to know
anything of what's really going on, is it, Mother?

[Good heavens! That's *exactly* what I was just saying!]

262
But consider, Eve! So many millions of us
have managed that huge task already –
(at every further routine second) – whether
we felt [uniquely?] terrified – or perhaps
could feel nothing – gone absolutely forever in any case –

[Death, surely? ("There's something very funny about the fact that other
people are mortal, isn't there?" (*Learmont*.))]

263
What, Beatrice? All these innumerable ancestors
managing life together with such difficulty
in order to develop precious *me*? I hardly think so!
How few of them, for instance, would even begin to understand
the first thing I was saying – however ancient the cliché?

[Oh, indeed. And how few others do even now!]

264
"But I too have wandered through a sort of jungle
for years, Dank, here, for years –
meeting no-one –
well, no-one much worth talking to, at any rate –
and they don't much like me here anyway – or so I find!"

265
In fact, darling,
I very much suspect
that they might *all*
have been flirting with me
during the sorry old political halfwit's funeral.

262
"The whole Universe, to my eyes (Dar),
seems to be a sort of major unholy accident
which has already happened. Oh well. Fair enough.
And yet: what are we supposed to be in all this?
The witnesses, perhaps? (But I saw next to nothing!)"

263
"Yes. So much of what we do
even here, Dandes – don't tell anyone else I said this –
are only the actions of those valiantly pretending
to be in something like command
of what existence may just possibly be."

[Yes. All existence – at least, all conscious existence – is itself a delusion of
grandeur. So my wise and beloved father often used to say anyway – and
who should know if not he or him?]

264
And all these almost infinitely subtle and spiritual
performance tasks in life and the various arts –
which, in old age,
can (it turns out) no longer be achieved
simply because of mere crude increasing physical weakness!

265
Only decades later
did it finally occur to me
that the expression on her face then
was surely more one of pride
than of any other emotion [– even including lust].

266
Really, Eve? Good Heavens!
I have known you
for several years now
without ever remotely
even suspecting that!

267
Or did I choose the wrong woman
ultimately? (Or, for that matter, perhaps even
right at the start?) (A ridiculous remark, Evie!
And I apologise for it again – although,
for obvious reasons, never *quite* sincerely.)

['What else could the All be? Whatever it changes into, it is still Itself.'
(Some Zeno or other.)]

268
Well, I chose her.
I have no-one but myself
to blame, I suppose.
I mean, you can hardly blame someone else
for existing, can you? (Well. Can you?)

[Of course, I have changed a lot of the names here – largely to
protect the san[ct]ity of the non-Existent.]

266

No, of course not; of course not;
nothing to do with your life
could be at all ridiculous, my Eve.
I wasn't thinking of something else.
No, really. I wasn't. Not for a single moment.

267

For is there really any much more
to even the highest life, my Penelope,
than primary moments? And in the best of them
more than a world of epics crushed together
could, even if successful, possibly hold –

[Bear in mind: 'There is no such thing as a successful literary epic.'
(Demcritus.) And perhaps also: 'There is no such thing as a successful
literary anything.' (Demnax.)]

268

and if, for instance, you had chosen
(perfectly reasonably) not to reply
to a clumsy remark in a huge reference library –
[millions of words – all those millions of words –]
none of those millions of words, my Eve,
which we have exchanged over exactly three decades –

[The quality of 'excerptness' here is once again deliberate of course. (By
the way, I have often thought that *A Clumsy Remark in a Huge Library*
would be the perfect title for any autobiography of mine – (this sounds
exactly like me talking, doesn't it?) – and, indeed, of quite a few of the
other people I know. Not that I know many other people, of course.
Entirely through my own choice, I need hardly add – (yet, nonetheless, for
some arcane and completely non-understood reason, do add anyway.)]

269
yet, almost for the most part
I cannot actually remember
the order the events happened in –
even of my own life! (who else's?)
one assumes they had an order –

[or is even that too much to assume?]

270
but then, if I have understood these latest, no doubt
substantially correct theories correctly, Adam –
I dare say the entire Universe
must always to a certain extent
be at the very least slightly ahead of its time. (No?)

["For what else, Suan, is the most accurate internal record of a lived life, if
not an escaping chaos of wildly anachronistic memories?"]

271
Millions and millions and millions and millions and millions
of years later,
an ecstatic child in a toyshop
says to his father; "No, Dad –
I think I like that red dinosaur the best."

272
Ah yes, indeed! The dinosaurs [the exotic non-dancers]! –
How many millions of years was it they had then? –
and how near did they ever get, do you think,
to producing a surge which got anywhere near Love?
[Well? How near do any of us ever get even yet?]
(Never?) And how big a failure for them, Eve, tell me, was that?

269

How is it I have now listened to you breathing
for minute after minute at night –
occasionally interrupted
by the sound of some bafflingly superfluous vehicle
speeding by to some other [non-]centre of the Universe –

270

Lived for millions of years
and never even for a moment
had an inkling of what they objectively were!
Not a suspicion about their complex, subtle hearts
or the sun itself, or the stars. (And as for love! – (or music!)

[But why music? And is this not to some extent true of everything living,
Dagmar? (Sorry – Deirdre.)]

271

Ah, yes! One thinks, indeed, of the dinosaurs –
banging so thunderously about for all those millions of years –
so hugely successful – without, as far as I can see,
having had the single least clue. Not even a hint
of theory as to what all or anything might be about.

272

"You know, this place seems to be absolutely full of people,
Beatrice, who had hardly the beginnings of the first clue –
but who somehow managed to survive and even thrive
often with a quite ludicrous degree of success – "
"Oh, it's not remotely what I expected, Dan, I admit."

273

But now that you are (or so I am told) dead, Beatrice,
I find that I have grown – the old story, I dare say –
to love you unreservedly. Easier that way, I know.
And it also demonstrates, at the very least, I admit,
even worse [male] emotional timing than usual.

[Perhaps the real one is always too complex?]

274

All those beautiful streets – their nearby woods –
a couple of wildly enchanting cities! – in which
so many other people were always already living –
(most of the vibrant details you still missed anyway of course) –
(not that the many cemeteries there were ever empty either) –

275

Yes. So much – thanks to the superfluous delight
of having a couple of kind relatives
to help you out! – (they did not need to be there –
did you?) – for a while at least a little more
swirls right round you and dazzlingly disappears!

276

Look there! other people
are travelling by, it seems, almost in boredom
through routine scenes which are still
so newly enchantingly new to me! –
and in such nonchalant, well-informed crowds too –

277

Yet, Adam, it is always only real limited people
making these their specific decisions
in actual places
out of their own hopes,
knowledges and inadequacies –

273

"No, my other one, it's not
remotely what I had envisaged either –
but there you are, I suppose.
Maybe it never is. I simply
chose [to be] the wrong person, might that be all it is?"

[Hard to see how it could be, Sweetheart.]

274

Even the smallest cemetery here, darling,
has so many as it were holes
down which one can pour away
more life than any of our
dazzling recording devices could ever carry.

275

On this remote German forest path
probably no-one else is at present walking.
And, even more likely, no one
is slowly bleeding to death anywhere
just to either side of it either.

276

And what of the slight air of surprise, Eden –
at finding out that foreign cities
are really there! – yes! – really here! My God!
All these windows! These cakes and recollections
(so often inaccurate) of historical incidents!

277

"Oh, yes – and all those innumerable f*cks, my darling,
which have happened to produce all of us! –
thousands – inter-caught millions of them, involving
people we would by and large prefer to be seen dead
rather than have the least living thing to do with! No?"

278
You know, it rather seems
that some folk pretty much knew this
right from the start, Eve –
why then did it take me so long
even to begin to grasp it?

279
"Oh, I fear at times
I too may have misunderstood
the whole effing thing,
darling. Certainly it's not
remotely what I had expected either."

280
"Yes, Evam, of course
we should try to improve
things. (You particularly.) Though probably
not absolutely everything at once,
eh? Hmm. Oh! Who baked that beautiful apple tart?"

281
"Do you really want my wisest advice, Dan?
Okay. Here it is. Do the best you can – right now –
where you actually are! Got that? Do it right now!
So. Is that any use to you? Not much? No?
Hmm. Have I maybe said this before?"

[Even so – I *hope* we don't intend to give up quite so easily?]

282
Very well then. Love! Be good! Feel compassion rather than hatred!
Try to treat absolutely everybody fairly! And ... er ... erm ...
(Oh God, God, God! If I could only have thought
of *one more piece of advice*, then this could easily have been
just about the greatest moral and political poem ever! No?)

278
"Short life – long life – who gives a f***, Dan?
It all ends and, after it all has ended,
here we are – I mean – not even here
able to say we aren't even here. All right. So.
What is anyone supposed to make of all *that*, Master?"

279
"And have you met her
charmless brute of a husband?
Somehow or other
he's managed to get in here
[too! I *can't* understand how.]
too! I can't *understand* how."

280
Actually, darling, it took me
almost a full month to finish
the second bottle you left!
But then again – I was abroad
for most of that time, I suppose, yes. Yes.

281
"In fact, I finished off the bottle
in just over a week, thank you, Eve –
while I was still trying to work out
what occasion could be quite special enough
to merit my opening it. [Then it occurred to me:
No time – (excuse my language) – like the present!]"

282
Though I quite like the idea, say,
of taking an adept shot at
an aspiring dictator
before he could cause the deaths
of, say, several million [by and large slightly boring] people.

283

Yes, indeed, my dear Beatrice, I can't say it too often.
Try to be good, my dear young b*nt – for it is better
to be good than to be bad. And there thou art!
(I hope no-one will now dare repeat the silly claim
that my work is morally neutral. But, if so: f*** 'em rigid!)

284

Anyway. What more do you f***ing
need to know, darling? Act accordingly.
Everybody else
is in this same mess too – more or less –
or whatever the f*** it more exactly is.

285

"Oh, yes, dear. I was left magnificently free
to get on with it, more or less
without any interruption
from anybody, for years on end! Yes.
My profoundest thanks to all concerned. No; really."

286

Tonight, Eve, I shall probably finish reading yet another
alleged masterpiece of so-called World f***ing Literature –
and shall no doubt fling it too contemptuously across the room
with a measured, humane and (I hope) essentially humble cry
of: "What a sanctified casket of lethal old galloping diarrhoea!"

283
Dreaming of a strangely
troublesome passage of arms, Helen – I woke up
to discover an old girlfriend of mine
diligently trying to cut off
my male member! (Ha! How we laughed! (Eventually.))

.

284
"She caused me a couple of years
of acute misery, darling – and for what?
Because I was a decent person?
I mean to say: I *did* try
so hard sometimes *not* to be!"

285
Is it not the case that human society
should or could easily be a lot better
than it actually is? Yes. Yes, of course it should.
And tell me, darling, why do you keep buying
such profoundly f***ing unflattering underwear? Eh?

286
"You know, if that really was his wife
who was sitting beside the newly appointed Professor
while he was giving his inaugural lecture on *Oedipus Rex*,
then, in my opinion, Benedikt,
he ought to be a very worried man."

287

"Do I have an opinion about the *Divine Comedy*, darling?
Well, yes, of course I do. Perhaps the most impressive
example, I should say, particularly nearer the start,
of the verbally magnificent confidence-trick. Still, at least
he didn't *quite* try to pass it off as Scriptural Truth, did he?"

[Yes. Do try to remember that this one here is also perfectly capable of *just
making things up!*]

288

"For a very great part of intellectual maturity,
I think, Emno, simple enough as it sounds, consists
in not being entirely submissive in the secure face
of ultra-confident assertion. Is that not right? No?
When dealing with real people at least it is, I think, a starting-point."

289

Hmm. Fascinating though
your opinions on posthumous existence
no doubt are, Professor Dogman –
may I ask you if you are truly unaware
that your expensive pullover is in fact on back-to-front?

290

"No. My dear Beatrice, after I have died,
exactly the same sort of plausible people who did
more or less nothing for me [or less] during my life
will reap from what I laboriously achieved a personal advantage
which few if any shall question their right to exult in. Just wait and
    see!"

287
"And surely it is to the immense credit
of the ancient Chinese – or to some of them at least –
that they never did quite do to Confucius
more or less what the Greeks did, with a nice reluctance,
to that other self-dramatising old nuisance Socrates?"

[Please note – assuming you even exist – (no offence!) – that I very much
wish to dissociate myself from these and such as these remarks. Mind you,
there is certainly something very weird about Confucius, I admit. One
takes it pretty much for granted – and I speak as one who has loved an
imaginary China for at least the last forty years – that if that incomparable
Johannes Factotum had ever had the actual rule of anything, be it so little
as a children's picnic, it would have resulted in utter disaster. (Perhaps
especially that, in fact.)]

288
Rereading, in growing mystification,
almost a dozen very warm old letters
that seemed so crucially important at the time –
I hear a close relative
farting in the kitchen downstairs.

289
using the large battered old copy
of *Time Regained*
as a makeshift paperweight –
even though it must be – what? –
at least five years since I last read it! –

290
oh, nothing much, darling – just sitting here doing my best
quietly working away, not greatly troubled, while waiting
presumably for the end of a personal universe
or the arrival of an otherworldly success –
whichever happens to get here first, you know?

291
"And how important is it, my dear Colleague,
that we are all, we must fairly suppose, going to die?
But, on second thoughts – please, don't bother answering.
No. You're probably only guessing anyway. Let's see.
Just try to do something even *mildly* useful instead! Eh?"

292
So. How could it have got into the boxes in this attic –
which neither of them ever learned of in his entire life –
this marvellously improving book, inscribed long ago
by an uncle whom I spent only a little time with
to a grandparent who died shortly before I was born?

[Hmm. God, as they say, only knows – (the uncle in question was a priest
for a while) – though I dare say one could manage a fairly intelligent guess
or two. But after a thoughtful moment, I throw it out anyway.]

293
But off we stream through life anyway, habitually chasing
what is surely so often a misconception bred in us
more than anything else, Adam, by the unique
unconditional, perhaps even excessive love
which parents directed towards us during our childhood!

294
Still, very many of them do try their best, I suppose –
But still, they don't do terribly well, do they, darling?
And where do all these decisions lead to anyway?
A fairly stupid question, I suppose. Is it? Never mind.
I'll try not to keep [you] awake for much longer – no –

291
What's that, Adam?
Everybody really was trying his or her
best? (Near me?) Dear me!
Have you ever heard anything *quite*
so depressing? Yes?

292
Still there, neatly packaged, on the kitchen table this morning –
that unused old Nazi postage-stamp which I now more and more
        think
we shouldn't have bought, no matter how *günstig* it was. No. What
lethal news might it so nearly have come with? Or what
innocent letter might it just not – (why not?) – have been used for?

[don't believe a word of it]

293
"As far as I can gather, Evechen,
it was losing all he had in some deliberated
disaster – including all his nearest and dearest –
which finally (perhaps in self-defence?) convinced him
of the essential if often elusive deep goodness of Providence."

294
"Whenever you lie down like that, Marey,
with your strong, somewhat p[l]easant knees up and apart
and your routine halo left so vulnerable and unguarded –
suddenly it no longer seems at all puzzling to me
that Almighty God should have made [at least some of] the
        decisions he did."

295
"Oh, Dian – truly I was in such distress for days –
I would have done absolutely anything to make it stop –
except of course finish it! For that would have been *a sin*.
So, in the end I took the wise advice of God's Son, you know –
and I cut them all off. Yes. Every last stupid effing one of them."

296
"Oh, god, yes Darling, all these
supposed omniscient beings who can nonetheless
so often be so easily manipulated
by silly equivocations and plays-on-words – at least
our own Three-and-One there is above that sort of nonsense!"

297
"Well, Dan, provided he is not forced
to alter his routine
even in the slightest, I should say
the Almighty Father has no rooted objection to –
well – to more or less anything! [How could he have?]"

298
So, darling. Once again we have
lasted into tomorrow (I
think). It gets easier and
easier doesn't it? Yes, er –
Hello. Erm. And who are you *exactly*?

299
Ah, yes – the great moments of one's youth!
They'll never come back again, I don't suppose.
Well, how could they?
I'm not there any more. In fact, Adam,
[I'm not sure I'm even quite here.]
I'm not sure I ever quite *was* there.

295

"Anyway, darling, I have burned or otherwise
destroyed all the photographs, so you need not ask
for any of them back – I have certainly
shown them to no-one else. How could I? Nobody –
but *nobody*, is interested in that sort of thing these days."

296

"Anyway, I have kept all these wonderful souvenirs for so long,"
said God, "that I can no longer remember
what it is they are meant to remind me of. Adam? Eve? Sin?
Obviously, Dad, I don't want to throw them out again –
at least not till I remember quite why I've kept them."

297

"Oh, *Maestro*, I seem to have
this terrible ability to recall more or less
every single foot I have ever put wrong! –
if only I could have been a psychopath –
[rather than, evidently, some sort of miraculous millipede –]
(like almost everyone else in these so-called higher circles) – "

298

"such a small intermittent swarm of
little regrets, regretchens, regretlets,
irritating me each moment of the day –
oh, thank God, *Maestro*, I have no
serious matters on my conscience – "

299

"Indeed, Eve, I dare say
at times I was even loved.
Yes. Or just about loved.
[We both have our own designs.]
Or would you deny me even that?
Oh, listen! The front door is opening yet again!"

300
"No, I can't quite work out – [" (said God)
"]whether I've lately broken through
into a new realm entirely –
or have merely, as it were,
fallen off the high-wire altogether."

301
There was something else – was there not? –
surely. What on earth was it? Ah, yes! Yes!
Yes, yes, yes! Yes, I remember now!
(Really, Adam, nobody has any idea
how much sheer bloody *work* there is in all this!)

302
matter keeps blossoming out
into a mind like this –
mine – or yours? –
with all those non-existent near misses
shearing off everywhere into [non-]abysses

303
"Sometimes they seem to be
even bigger, Adam,
than anything we ourselves
will ever manage to reach to –
if you know what I mean."

304
"Well, I should hope not.
Obviously.
But, beyond that, well,
Penelope, I'm afraid I
just don't really know."

300

"Oh, no. It was still
happening. I just wasn't
able to see it
out of the particular
hole or abyss in question."

301

Somehow or other these distances
always take me by surprise
more and more
with every passing year –
(but I still didn't see you there!)

302

Oh, we should have got them to talk about it
while they were still here –
but we didn't.
What on earth
were we always talking about instead?

303

You're ten minutes late!
But when you shut the outside door
our great history at last
seemed to emit its final gasp (not before time, dear!)
then keeled over and died completely unlamented –

304

For if even five seconds ago
it had all suddenly stopped –
yes – dead. Gone. All gone.
So what? Well, my angel?
What do you hear now? (Eh?)

305
in fact what I now regret
is not that I was perhaps too indiscreet –
but rather that, through sheer incompetence,
I missed so very much – you know? –
of the really vital stuff out.

306
These days, in fact, darling,
I try more and more
to keep my once rampant imagination
under severe control. (Oh, if only Almighty God
had originally chosen to do the same!)

307
"What else did I ever want?
What more can I say?
How ridiculous it all was!
Simply too ridiculous
to make one want to be more specific now."

308
"I doubt if even a glorious mortal heart
can take all a strain like this for much longer,
Beatrice. Perhaps you had better
retreat some little way into the other realm
where I can't make out quite so much of you?"

309
"But remember, darling. Only through Space–Time,
is Space–Time conquered. And thus may we be led
forever onward (or for a decent while
at least – till the stars slam shut) by the unchanging-
transient – my dazzling mystic, invisible (excuse me) *anus*!"

305

"The most important thing here is –
but what important thing is there really?
this, Adam? that? the next thing?
not an infinite line of important things
off in every direction whatsoever?"

306

"Enough that such sublime moments
did happen too! That (perhaps) is that.
And to me as well! No. To us! To us!
However, even as it is, it's nearly
all other people, isn't it, darling? No?"

307

"Tell them absolutely nothing about us, Adam –
in matchless verse or prose, whichever
suits your needs best. For absolutely nothing
is exactly what these rejoicers of other times deserve
or want or need to know. And now, if you'll excuse me … "

308

"As for me, all I really want to do
is run around Paradise for all eternity, shouting
little else but "——! ——! ——!""
"Forever, darling? Don't you think that's a bit
immature? (Not to mention, repetitive.)"

309

"Look, Beatrice – er, look, Penelope, sorry –
or whatever your name is – Eve, is it? – no, listen.
Oh, for God's sake, why all this sudden
flouncing around? – aren't you lot pretty much
the same person anyway? Oh, *for God's sake*, darling!"

310
"But women are absolutely wonderful whereas men
are shits, Dante – surely more or less everybody
knows that by now? It's all a part of how
we're different and yet equal – though with women
routinely tending to be slightly better, if anything. No?"

311
"Shit! I can't even get
the f★★★ing thing started this morning
at all!" – complained Almighty God
with a somewhat practised captivating grin
to someone or other. (Surely not his delightful Mother?)

312
"Are you sure you're all right?"
"Yes, thanks. Yes, I'm very happy now."
(And yet the next morning
I didn't even hear the sound
of the front door shutting.)

313
Oh, I'm finished, I'm afraid.
God, yes. More or less finished.
(On the other hand, my dear Penelope –
how can this have happened
when I never quite managed to get started?)

314
That wonderful day, for instance, when she sat down
at the edge of the bed, and said in laughing disbelief:
"How amazing! That's almost *five full months*
you've been here already! Do you still think it's a dream?"
What did I say in reply to that? (Surely not nothing?)

310
I don't know. Somehow women
are always vaguely
at the very least reminding me
of other women. (Yes, Eve.
And often of something else too, I admit.)

311
Could you not have helped me
a little bit more, darling?
Or even, for that matter,
a little bit less? No? Either
might well have been just enough.

312
It is all unthinkable –
but a little of it gets thought anyway.
What may all this not do?
And, having somehow done it,
what more may it not do next?

313
no static bliss – of any sort
for anyone – in any future –
nor past – nor misery, for that matter;
past clouds – slow clouds – slower clouds?
that's all there is to it anywhere (my unique love!)

314
"No, Stranger, listen. There is nothing else to inhabit
but the real world you seem so keen to fly from. Nothing!
There's only that vast everything all around you – inside and out –
the physical stuff, you know? The supposed non-physical
is merely the more elusive side of the physical. And that's that."

315

"Look – I'm sorry to have to tell you this, Dan.
Perhaps I should have done so earlier. But – erm – well –
I'm not Beatrice." "You're not?" "No. Not really."
"What do you mean, *not really*?" "Well. Not at all, in fact.
It's the same old story. You know? Frankly, you've got the wrong
    void."

[It's probably the human condition, is it not?]

316

"Absolutely not.
No, dear. No.
Nothing at all. Not unless
I've just forgotten the whole damn thing!
And what, realistically, are the chances of that?"

317

"Yes indeed. We are here anyway.
This one is the other world after all, darling.
This is the other one after all.
Perhaps this is the real one after all!
Yes. And the seeming one is the only real one."

318

Well, what else can [we] you do?
So long as some of it is true at least –
that's as much as [you] we can hope for,
I suppose. Of course, there cannot be more truth, Beatrice,
than there is a Universe to hold it. Can there?

[No. Don't be so bloody stupid.]

315
Wrong? Wrong? Of course I could be wrong!
I could be wrong. You could be wrong. *Anyone*
could be wrong at any time. So what? The Impossible
remains impossible for all that − (although I grant you
we may also be wrong in what we think is impossible!)

316
"That it should nonetheless
flood on so gloriously like this
through the rest of our
lives, Adam! That's
what − er − hello?"

317
"I'm not just talking
about the ancients here, Eves!
No. No − far from it!
People die. People are born.
We're smeared out a bit. That's all."

318
And all theories of life which are not based
on us coming and going − *really*
coming and *really* going − vanishing −
are evading the deepest issues, my darling.
(Mind you: who can quite blame them?)

[*I* blame them! Yes. I blame them too!]

319
Unable, my darling, to predict
with certainty even how loud
our next fart will be – we nonetheless
tell ourselves such lovely little stories
as to what this unbounded business is really all about!

320
Just throw one box of them
onto another, my treasure –
and then get rid of them all!
It turns out they don't matter. No.
(No-one will miss them in the least.)

["[Ultimate] Reality, my dear Mr Jekklefechan, is simply a name which
some of us prefer to give to what just happens to be here."]

321
"Yes. That'll be my next move.
I'll just burn all this rubbish, Beatrice –
then simply disappear.
It's the least I can do.
They'll be *so* grateful for it."

322
Oh, I dare say no-one
is *more* important – or could be –
but I am not really
all *that* important, am I? (And yet,
these clouds and bushes here routinely talk to me!)

323
"God said – er no, not God –
you know, the other one, darling. Or, rather –
no. Not the other one.
No. I mean – well, okay – fine – all right – yes.
Maybe not one of them actually said it. No?"

319

Ah yes. Overwhelming images
of the vast surrounding darkness.
Very nice. Yes.
You certainly caught it there, Master.
(And all at such reasonable prices too!)

320

In the end, that's pretty much all there is to it.
The as-if-endless screaming of innumerable birds
on a vast, sheer rock in the ocean –
with no great being immaterially watching on
and nobody counting even as far as ten.

[Or, for that matter, Odysseus, even as far as one? ("The Universe itself,
Oenone, cannot count further than one." (*St Geminius*)).]

321

Beyond the hotel, I turned the corner
and suddenly realised what was wrong.
The Moon! The Moon was simply far too big!
Swollen to four or five times its proper size
it hung (it seemed even to sway!) very close to the island.

322

Oh yes, in all that
period of my life, as far as
I remember, Eve, I was permanently
more or less off my head – because of something
or other or, you know, I forget these days quite who – er, quite what.

323

Again and again, it seems,
she set me much the same test – perhaps
to see whether, this time, I might at last
manage to [pass?] fail it. But, it looks as if
I never quite succeeded in doing so.

324
Yes, I went through a phase
of suspecting that only I
existed, Adam, but –
something or other –
what the hell was it now? –

325
(And then again, what
would be *too much* to expect
from someone in any way like
Him, darling – or It –
I freely admit! Have I gone yet?)

326
"But where else could it go to
and at what other time? When else could it be now?
Did I say the right things to you? did I perhaps do
what I should have done? What else am I meant to think?
Anyway, all the best moments will [also] be forgotten then too."

327
"But I fear that, for the flies and fleas and so forth
even our greatest deep achievable genius
would be, in long time, just one more convenient part
of the vast inter-connected material food chain
which the universe offers, Eve, or even is."

324

"Well, Beat, couldn't He have created folk who both
had Free Will, yet somehow always made
the right decisions *anyway*? It hardly seems too much
to expect from someone who could do absolutely *anything*.
Or can't I ever quite understand that yet either, Darling?"

325

Oh yes –
I can see myself doing it
easily enough –
though not quite
at the moment, Danley, perhaps!

326

"No – wait a minute yet – no – I'll miss this place –
all the high-class thrashing around – yes – and
why does it take us so long to find out
that we know almost nothing at all
about this about that about – even dying in Heaven –

327

"But then, what else is Reality to be?
What have I learnt? Oh, not so much general
appreciation – no, my dear – than [then?] sheer death – eternally
predictable but surprising – whenever
the world as it might perhaps be has simply moved on."

[These sound to me like somebody's last words, Vitie?
(In fact, they sound to me like almost *anybody's* last words.)]

328
Hidden away for safety in the attic
the rather fine old picture of the Crucifixion
is now somehow being eaten away
by a colony of larvae – which (of course)
do not for a moment know what they are doing.

[Yes, well, if they aren't larvae, Kay, then they are no doubt something
else.]

329
"Those vicious, indiscriminate little contributors! –
what did they think they were doing, working away like that,
causing such a commotion in my poor,
beleaguered insides? What did they think I was?
Friend? Enemy? No thought? Nothing whatsoever?"

330
These clouds! These crowds! What do they think they are doing?
Well. Nothing, obviously. No such thought
occurs to them. No thought of any kind
occurs to them. Not even, I suppose –
(what? *none* of them think?) – that they are a sort of *them*.

331
Of all that the moments I remember best are, say –
simply getting on and off the routine, scheduled trains.
Bright glimpses of the ordinary lives
which I am being an enchanted tourist through
for perhaps only this precarious day and the next.

[Yes. That ordinary but unforgettable stroll along from Berg, for instance.]

328

"But we are not faded things which somehow
'passed through' real life, Eve. (As if we were not
just as much an imbrued and involved part of it all
as anything else is!) – any other real detail,
a speck of ancient insect or a sheer hurtle of stars – "

['Imbrued', Beatrice? 'Fated'?]

329

Such vapours of innumerable lives inside us all! –
[our thoughts too?] –
and not for a moment a single suspicion anywhere
of who we are. (Or anything else, for that matter.
Who *they* are, for instance.) [(Who are you, by the way?)]
Perhaps, Eve, we should try to talk to the neighbours a bit more?

330

While I was coming back on
a train out to the distant airport –
a fly landed on my arm!
What thoughts was it possibly having? (Any?)
And what of my own great thoughts during that melancholy trip?

331

Let's see, darling. When you swat a fly
it is only one part of the Universe
interacting with another – no? – pretty much the same
as if the fly were to kill you. (Or one of us. Which, indeed,
has happened time without known number so far, has it not?)

[Presumably a reference to near unimaginable number of human beings
who have died directly because an insect bit them. (Berg, for instance.)]

332
The train happened to stop while facing
a perfectly ordinary little path into the woods –
which I could see no-one walking on.
Then, after perhaps a minute or two,
[it started to move away again.]
just as it started to move away again –

333
Two obvious lovers
waiting in the small bus station
right at the edge of town –
where a small deep path runs into or out of
the clutch of dark trees just beyond them.

[Just look at that, Gretchen! The same (small) word twice!]

334
Always, my darling, there are other trains
taking off for elsewhere. Does it much matter
which particular station we are in?
But, you know, I rather think these stairs here
ought to lead us straight back up to the car park.

[((Is this perhaps Paisley too?) Partick? Paris? Passport Control?]

335
"Hmm. This message roughly scratched
onto the innermost wall – look! can't you see it? –
of such a long-since abandoned religious
institution says something, Ivie, which
no doubt does a great deal to explain its abandonment."

332
That chap beside me in the last carriage
was almost certainly carrying an extra head –
but I do hate starting up a conversation
with strangers on trains and so forth
if I can possibly avoid it. (Like most people, I suppose!)

333
"No. No more, Eve, than walking down various streets
to and from various bright and pleasant shops –
Oh, yes. An occasional palace too, perhaps!
Just missing – or just catching – the right connection.
Time? Well, what more is Time supposed to be doing?"

["Time does nothing. It derives from the doing itself." (*The Book of Chang E.* VII, 13, e, 10)]

334
Do you think that pair were having an argument
when they strode past us outside the station in Partick?
(Were they joking?) I couldn't quite work it out. Could you?
("Particularly given" – he said – "that Time is always
such a f★★★ing precarious concept anyway, darling.")

[And don't you think, Polly, that might not have been us?]

335
"Yes, very well, darling. But do please take care.
Above all, don't get onto the wrong train now.
And then perhaps get off at the wrong station,
somehow turning into the right life
which should in fairness be someone else's. Okay?"

336
Admiring in disbelief the astonishing
riot of stars out last night, unfortunately,
I fell right off the suburban balcony [and died!]. Still,
technically, I suppose I shouldn't really
have been out there in the first place, should I, darling?

337
But suddenly I staggered and fell to the ground –
hit, most probably by a large, jaggy stone
thrown in from a neighbouring garden by
some unruly angel or drunk. Let's see. (Hmm. These things
nearly always lend themselves to *profound* misinterpretation.)

338
"This was, truly, a worthy adversary. Indeed
I still have one of his legs buried, I think,
in my own garden. His head too, I suspect.
Though I admit, Doddelius, I am not entirely
sure of this. No. I would have to check it first."

339
("Do I perhaps
still say 'I'
a little too often?
Sorry, my Beatrice.
But that too should soon pass.")

340
"Oh just forget these miracles, eternal insights, secret powers!
Ego fantasies, Don – mere attempts to cope with the fact
that in the seemingly endless real world, you – yes, even
the great, unique you – are one more of the ignorant infinite dots
rather than the vast central vortex we must feel ourselves to be."

336

"You know, when first I came to live beside this lane
some (dear God!) thirty-odd years ago already –
I little suspected, my divine Andromeda,
that eventually someone not yet even technically born
would come here too to run [ruin?] my life!"

337

Oh, look! – yet more nice houses here.
More fairly nice people living in them
for years too, I dare say –
in this narrow, enclosed road beyond the train-station
where we whiled away a few more superfluous minutes.

338

"But perhaps the world will merely end first –
yes – that would be more fitting – before it rots away
where I have buried it in the tiny garden
behind the house where I almost bound you with it.
Ha! Pardon my little joke, O Daughter of Eildone, Dare and Li!"

339

"I dare say, if life has taught me anything
(not that it necessarily has, O Agamemnon)
it's that you can never be too careful, can you?
(Although, now I come to think about it –
actually you *can* sometimes, can't you?) Hmm."

340

"As for love, if I understand it aright,
I think we must take it that the huge advantages
somehow outweigh the not unhuge disadvantages –
or am I perhaps being, as so many up here are,
just a little too romantic again, my dead darling?"

341

"Know [No?], Fair Stranger. I knew only one of my parents –
also only one of my formerly resonant grand-parents –
and, needless to say, none of all those who went before.
No, scarcely a single detail of all those lives beyond
who had gone to constitute me. (Not that they ever quite mean to!
    Eh?)"

342

I would very much like
to have had children, Eve –
but I didn't!
On the other hand,
so very many other people did.

343

"My children are not quite my children.
My spouse is not quite my spouse.
And even these fine rooms around me
are somebody else's mirror, darling,
which will not quite show my own true face."

[Triplets?]

344

Yet there is a little too much
of the air of obsolete coinage
about the stars sometimes, Adam –
if you see what I mean. No? Compared
(say) to those bright windows over there? Not so?

345

Why do I so love this flat, Lea? Well –
chiefly because it contains my wife's eyes,
I suppose. In fact, incredibly enough –
at the moment, it contains absolutely all of her!
(Unless she's just slipped out in the last half-hour, of course.)

341
"Oh I probably *should*
have married her – yes, yes – and to Hell with it!
I mean to say, what a beautiful, er, you know,
beautiful *nature* she had. Yes. But wait! Oh, God!
Just a moment! Wait! That was you too, wasn't it?"

342
What? Three of them
at exactly the same time?
Good Heavens!
Who would have thought it?
It all sounds quite impossible to me.

343
But perhaps to die
much as one has lived –
[in a place one did not
ever quite feel perfectly at home in –]
in a place which very often
one did not feel particularly at home in –
even though it was our only *possible* home –

344
Were it not for a sudden change of plan
I would probably be travelling
down the coast on a busy train this morning –
not sitting here like this near a bay window
vaguely watching the [busy] traffic pass by on Highburgh Road.

345
Morning. Hello. You still
do not know
what has been written
on the back of the universe,
do you, my angel?

346

Darling, was it you
who jotted this down
on the back of the calendar? –
some time last year, I suppose.
Because it *certainly* wasn't me.

347

Oh God no, please –
you are going to have to put
your petrol-effect silk blouse back on again at once.
For look! Time is at the kitchen window – and I fear
this mor[Eve]ning he may have brought a proper lawyer along.

348

my God, I thought, it's true –
her large legs up on a kitchen chair –
beautiful, yes – but another form of life –
if long enough goes by – who can say enough –
and a sort of insect starts to write something down –

['Large'? Can this be quite right? Of course, one knows what is meant –
but wouldnt 'rangy' (or even 'gangling') catch it a bit better? Not to
mention a forthright, straightforward 'long'. Or, for that matter, 'magnifi-
cent', 'superb', 'enchanting'. Still, it's not much worse than 'big', I'll give
you that.]

349

"No. It's impossible to combine the language of adoring astonishment
(for want of a better phrase) with the crude, sexual and explicit.
You are wrong even to try, Sadam. It simply cannot be done.
Though, I concede, there may perhaps be a certain joy to be gained
from discovering quite how one cannot manage to achieve it."

346
Right here, V, in the narrow kitchen
of a woman whom I never intended to love
I –
er –
what? Again?

347
"Oh, I dare say it's rather like an endless calendar –
with some infinite pages unaccountably missing
and *such* a weak temporal sense. Yes, Adam.
Or – Yes, Eve. That's just about does it. We thought
it would never end – but it did! (Didn't it?)" (Well?)

[What? Did it end well?]

348
Why? Well, roughly because a sense of sheer moral goodness
radiates from her – I suppose – which (I suppose) dazzles me
perhaps even more than does the beauty of certain
maddening and complex little structures which (of course) are kept
hidden for most of the time – though never quite (strangely)
        unpresent.

[Not a neurological reference, I trust.]

349
"But we call and call at the top of a long, almost depthless well –
and when the echo returns to us – deep, confused, muffled –
we take it to be the uncanny voice of a vast being
saying to us something else, something immensely profound,
Eive, in its own not quite humanly intelligible language."

350

"But then, Dandan, I suspect
that most of us have views – often absolutely
central views – which utterly take for granted
what is not in fact even
statistically or technically possible. Yes, dear. That is true."

351

Oh, yes, yes. So much of it, Adam,
is a fight against, a shrieking at the near endless
assault on the ego – which needs to see itself
as central, as of unique importance to the universe – which it
isn't – (hence the scarcely bearable tension sometimes. No?)

352

"For what are most of the favourite spiritual profundities
but forms of self-flattery? More or less anything
which expresses in a sufficiently rich, sonorous way
the great resonating myth – that death isn't *really* death –
disappearance not true disappearance – will thus be venerated."

353

Yes! All those strange tongues wagging about –
the wide hope that uncanny secrets of the Universe
will somehow drop into our more or less hairy heads –
while our tongues and lashes flutter intelligently to and fro!
(And as if we should all be *somewhere else* even so!)

354

Only now, when I am right at death's door,
do I finally (and too late!) begin to understand
why the – but no! Wait! Wait! On closer inspection,
I'm probably not dying just yet, am I? Right.
Good. So. Let's see. What the f*** was I talking about?

350
"Some non-physical agent running it all from beyond-Beyond!
I mean to say that, Deirdre, is already bad enough –
who gives to us (to *us*!) his final commands
through some dreary old Jimmu or Bartab or whatever!
Did they really all believe that once? Really? Or even yet?"

351
"It's a fundamental
insight – without which
the real world can hardly even
begin to be
properly organised, darling."

352
Even so, in the end, what – (correct me, Eve,
if I'm wrong) – is all that sort of spiritual stuff
but a tempting delusion of personal centrality
combined with an at times (at best) wonderfully
creative and resonating abuse of language? Eh?

353
Oh, this unending hopeless nonsense
about somehow keeping on going somehow
after it has all so obviously drifted away!
You die, Adam, you're out of it, Eve, you're gone –
and that – whoever you are (or were) – is that!

354
"Some people, we know, did feel something at moments
which their words could not help them better with than to call
a sense of timelessness – but nothing in the processes
of the vast complex ever-working head is free of now
and then and next. No real mind is ever really timeless."

355

Let's see. Would you maybe rather belong
to some other place entirely?
Or to the opposite sex (bless 'em!)?
And perhaps already be dead?
Possibly, not yet alive? Eh?

[I wonder if maybe 'I' should be the pronoun in the first line.
(Indeed, on second thoughts – forgive the repetitiousness – but one rather
suspects that any pronoun whatsoever could be given there!)]

356

Believe me, darling, innumerable other people
will envy you your position in years to come.
Yes. All down the particularly relevant ages in fact.
I dare say that isn't noticeable just at the moment.
But then, not much is ever noticeable just at the moment, is it?

357

But do try to be good anyway, my dear –
for it is better to be good than bad.
And there you are. (You want even more?)
I hope no-one will now dare repeat the silly claim
that my work is morally neutral. (Or even worse!)

358

"Oh, what do most of them care much
about celestial masterpieces anyway?
I mean to say, why bother?
Hmm. Maybe I *am* dead, Eve.
Or have I simply grown a little bit taller?"

355
And the timeless living states which they invent for themselves –
up ahead – up ahead – always some way up ahead –
a glimpse of changeless survival forever – for them
or a sort or sept of them – these too are their sheer fantasies.
Any sort of real existence, Urum, must be based on real change.

[Um. Two different languages. (Well – how could they possibly be two *same* languages?)]

356
"But this is not an ideal world,
is it, my not-quite-perfect visitor?
What? Is it really?
Good Lord! How I wish someone clever
had told me that a little bit earlier!"

357
"Truly, I wonder how much, my dear Donde,
the spirits themselves are aware of this,
or admire it. And vice-versa, of course.
(If *vice-versa* in fact
can have any meaning here.)"

358
No. Unless I have blundered very badly.
I must be still alive.
Yes. Still alive!
Still alive! How did that happen?
(Mind you – how did *anything* happen?)

359

"How have I managed to keep myself alive
throughout all this long and troublous time? –
I wondered to myself. And then I finally grasped
the subtle objection, Ex(e). Maybe, in fact, I *hadn't*!
But, in that case, what was my actual alternative? Eh?"

360

"Indeed, Eve, it may be that some things
can never be fully recovered from –
(but is that not true of everything?) –
even though we could hardly
have got here exactly without them –

361

Waking up for a moment –
to see a sort of large monk[ey]
tiptoeing through the room!
A ghost, I suppose?
What? Not [even] a ghost?

362

Or are we a sort of intruder
into the world of beetles?
Not that it much matters:
no-one invited them in either –
I hardly think. (Well, who would?)

363

Who or what is that
crawling across the bathroom floor
so early in the morning?
(Of course, I would not normally
be in here at this time of day myself.)

359
For these quiet moments
on a quiet sublime morning
are exactly the same sort that even the greatest lived through
(wrapped round their own hardly known skeletons!) –
to get to wherever it is they have got to now.

360
Yes. Morning again. Her face
must be not far away from me
somewhere in a not yet quite arrived light
made up largely of love, hope and the future. So.
Is our strange chaotic past still here in the room too?

361
And yet, how else is anyone
ever to meet anyone? Is a God
perhaps to flutter down and perform
the necessary introductions? (And yet, Ave, surely
I was often waiting precisely for something like that!)

362
As far as I know, Dea,
the two most important people in my life
never once met each other.
Never even saw each other.
(Or did so by chance – and never suspected a thing?)

363
Six o'clock in the morning –
and I am out of bed again
though I don't have to be.
And another car goes rattling by
in the street below. (Hmm. Does it really *have* to?)

364

"[Eye,] I do not want still to be here
when whatever is in the ocean
at last comes back out of it.
No. I will gladly leave all that
to people with a lot more energy than myself."

365

"Look, darling! More of those fading
white lines in the sky –
and always with them a bright sense
that really it should be *me*
up there in the purer air!
[If 'air' is quite the right word here.]

366

"Oh, yes. I used to suspect" – (No, not really) –
"I would end up getting perfectly jaded with everything.
But, as it turned out, one or two things forced me
to fly from so restricted a view. However,
you don't really want to know what they are now, do you?"

[So, my matchless match. What next? Are we not all simply one more of
the numberless [self-]astonishing shapes which Matter (as it turns out) was
able to turn itself into? And stay there for a while?]

364

Hmm, thought Oedipus to himself, pondering the riddle.
"A crowd of people who don't or who hardly know each other –
and are then replaced by the same again. And again and again."
Let's see. A waiting queue? Or Life itself? Or why not: *Everything*?
Hmm. And why is the Sphinx suddenly showing her eavage to me?

365

in the end, (Fair Stranger), pretty much as usual,
women will decide most of it, and men
will think they have decided it – provided that
the whole damn thing has not already
seeped through yet another near- or non-hole in the sky –

366

not quite that the wisdom of Age (if any)
might have little or no application for the young –
or that it might even, O Oracle, be harmful!
(and not only for the young?
not much good for anyone, in fact?)

[Oh, all right, my better half. No doubt, never quite so simply. But what
next anyway? Can two perhaps, for instance, somehow really become one?
Yes? Very well then. One what?]

Three

1
it was right in this room here – wasn't it?
Yes, it was! How could I have
forgotten so soon?
But then – not all music sounds the same
even if it should do – (does it?)

2
And almost as if slightly above things –
behind, below, or to the side of it all –
the near-perfect music is always playing
at just the wrong speed, my darling,
in not quite the right room.

3
Yes. The near-perfect music is nearly always
playing at just the wrong speed
in not quite the right room –
and I can't say I am over-much impressed either
by the strangely mixed audience it has somehow managed to attract.

4
"Yes, darling – I can't help thinking sometimes
that when apes – or whatever they were back then –
started to ask "Yes, darling? Exactly why?"
then the whole damn thing began
to slide sideways just a little too quickly."

5

And after I had travelled, on rather a brilliant inspiration,
almost the whole length of the country, what
were the first words she greeted me with?
"Oh, hello there. No. You really
ought not to have come. *Somebody else* is here."

6

Oh well.
Maybe all
the other people who were involved in it
are dead by now, Evere. Yes.
One can but f***ing hope.

7

And yet, something like the tenuous voice
as of a recently defunct goddess
is still continually calling to me these days – I think
from that small cupboard up there above the
draining-board – (though never (*alas!*) by quite the right name.

8

For we do not wish to see, do we, Adam,
just how well others can get by
entirely without [either of] us.
(Which they almost always can do so –
as a matter of fact – *insultingly* easily.)

9

"Oh, foreign languages, you know,
aren't *nearly* as subtle, Van – we all just know that.
Much as those foreign buildings, well, you know –
well, you can hardly really live in them *at all*,
can you? You know? How do they manage it in fact?"

10

But all this afternoon, the noise of various people
using the lower flights of stairs in the building –
every last one of them surely some unique German? –
reaches me again and again in the attic flat
where I sit writing something in slightly the wrong language.

11

What are they all doing? Visiting the dentist?
Or perhaps the small, quiet lawyer – (who lives nearby)?
Or the (as yet never seen) specialist in (also unseen) internal organs?
From this attic flat right up at the top of the stairway
one can never quite be sure which door below is being used.

12

For some reason, still awake late that night,
another poorish and unknown K., in a German attic room
right next to a small main-street bookshop –
in the two front windows of which no doubt there yet stand
those huge sceptical-looking photographs of Kafka and Proust –

13

"Tell me – do you have anything sort of like a diary –
but leaning on Dante and Milton (or the Bible), with some nice
Greek myths interspersed throughout, more than a hint
of the *Psychopathia Sexualis*, I rather suspect – and the whole thing
built loosely on a quasi-Japanese superstructure? What? No?
       Not yet? Oh. Right."

14

The poet plunged into the dark German forest here
and was never seen again! – Well, not until
some thirty-five minutes later, when he emerged
from the other side of it, looking round himself, completely
lost – (though, in fact, only *just* beyond the town cemetery).

15

Listen. There is brass music being played at present
in the schoolyard directly across the road from us.
Meanwhile, an unknown man has gone away,
carrying your cracked kitchen window
to his van parked somewhere undeniably possible nearby.

16

"Consider, Eve, where they used to be for instance!
They used to be in your insides, did they not?
More children, eh? Oh, not for very long, I admit.
But how much personal preparation should we have
for a universe this size? A million years each, perhaps?"

[Personally – [Oh, God! he's back!] – I have always rather suspected that
the Universe is probably the unintended by-product of something else –
and quite possibly something of considerably less intrinsic importance. But
I dare say I may be wrong.]

17

Incredibly enough, you have a small technicality
out of which real life may quite conceivably come –
even though at this particular moment
you are sitting quietly elsewhere in this very room
reading a more or less lunatic book about prophecies.

(Life was obviously created in order to pander to some fairly disgusting
creature's vanity. I'll say no more here.)

18

Time, eh? Whatever hopeful batteries does the
world run itself up and down on if not
via these priceless minor folds? (There!) Up and down,
up and down, into sheer joy it goes, or whatever
monstrous wrong wish [fish?] swims into the wrong small net.

19
"My God, Yvo, what a birthday party that was!
Two of the coats – (though not, alas, the cats) – went missing.
Somebody broke the dirty big sculpture beyond repair.
The abstract poet fell down the stairs, drunk. (Oh, yes;
he survived – but you can't expect absolutely *everything* …

20
"All right, Mr Mozart. Well done. Well done indeed.
You have passed the audition. Well done. The job is yours.
And now, if you'll excuse us …
I dare say you'll understand; the fact is
we have other, you know, really *dreadfully* important things to do."

21
"What – me? Oh, I'm afraid I
slipped out at the interval, Adam.
I just felt, somehow,
I had better things to do,
you know? Anyway. How about you?"

22
Me? Oh, now the steam [stream?] of life, I feel,
has almost overwhelmed me –
almost borne me away
to a magical land just beside us –
(just beyond the supermarket car park?)

23
What was I doing the moment
before we met? (Sitting in a library –
reading something, was I?
Is that even possible? But what
real book could ever signal quite so much?)

24

"Oh, you'll probably find yourself strangely at home here, Dan.
At least those who dislike your latest productions
tend more and more to have to
express their hostility explicitly in this blessed place –
which is, you might say, progress of a sort, I suppose. No?"

25

"In fact, I believe that, even only last year,
it was extremely fashionable here all throughout the summer
for women to bring out those long rare wings
which they usually (for entirely understandable reasons) prefer to
    keep hidden
and flutter them languidly round themselves in street after street
    after street.

26

("Why? Well, how on earth should I know why
they did it? As the mood took them, I suppose.
I can't say I noticed it myself, I have to confess.
Some underling must have told me. Yes. I do have
important things to do in this place myself, you know?")

27

Good news, my fellow citizens of this nirvana!
Guess what! Yes! Last night I got to play for absolute *hours*
with her infinitely wonderful full big aristocratic
trumpeters! Hello? She didn't mind. Hello? Oh – come on!
Why all this feigned indifference? (Not jealousy, I hope? Not
    envy, I do so hope?)

28

"No. She was a quiet, rather boring woman, if anything –
or so I found. In fact, she came in here one evening,
showing a fairly startling amount of cleavage –
and it took me *hours*, Penelope, even to suspect
that there might have been something sexual about it."

29

But with what a stupid urgency we collapsed together!
yes, right there in the bright wide high-class modern kitchen –
while Helen's wise-idiot of a non-local husband
nipped smartly back to the nearby office, to search out
a book of old local photographs he so much wanted me to see! –

30

Such fascinating snippets of conversation
one hears in passing these days, darling,
(thanks to the mobile phone) –
"You know what your problem is, Mate, don't you?
What? What? No! What? Not even the women?"

31

"Why do you say that?" I asked her,
jokingly. "Do you perhaps want to marry me?"
To which she instantly replied:
"Yes."
A total and shattering shock, Eve, obviously.

32

TAKE CARE. THIS IS ALL MINE
said the beautifully decorated sign
high above the Great Infinite and Immortal Gate.
(Written, fortunately, Vee, in a beautiful language
which nobody else thereabout could quite understand.)

33

What? Poetry? Ah, yes! Well, let us then by all means
wamble on, Virgil, abusing language *so* creatively, making
exquisitely well-judged remarks about all the nice pretty colours
and how God talks to us – (Christ! I'm blissed!) – if only *sotto voce* –
whenever, say, the sunlight slants impressively enough through –

34

"Look. The chief justification for explicating poetry,
I suppose, my dear old Jadus, is that these explanations,
though often absurd, can be distinctly more interesting
than are the poems themselves. (Not particularly difficult
in most cases, God knows.) So then, Mate. How did you die *really*?"

35

Such interesting snippets of conversation
one hears in passing these days
thanks to the mobile phone –
"Actually, I suspect that all languages –
er – er – what? No. No, I can still hear you."

36

"What did you say? 'Innumerable insects
laying a single egg?' Yes. Striking, Adam, I admit. But does it
make any sense? Or perhaps I'm too old-fashioned? Yes.
So – don't give up your striking phrases yet, darling! Who knows
what great truths they may not somehow prove to be a *symbol* of?"

[Distrust more or less everything with the word 'somehow' in it.]

37

Time to go? But I sit on [t]here in the small park
and tear off another comparatively chance moment
from the vast, dangling bunch of them
which someone, or some not too unkindly nothing,
is still dangling so temptingly just in front of me.

38

And, nearby, while the kettle is again straining
triumphantly (for I would be triumphant!) to the boil –
I manage to – (if only just) – furtively pick up
enough of the new details here in the kitchen to persuade
the uncut universe not to turn its back on me yet again.

39

Let's sit down here for a bit first, eh?
Did you remember to bring the sandwiches –
that's the important thing. We can always go on
to see the Pictish Art Exhibition later – or tomorrow,
if need be. After all, it runs for another full week, does it not?

[The Picts were one of the more artistic and mysterious early indigenous
groups which inhabited Ireland. Or it may be England, I suppose. Or some
other bloody place entirely. The Andaman Islands, perhaps? (As if I partic-
ularly cared!)]

40

I scratch my itching back
with the first thing
that conveniently comes to hand –
Oh no!
Oh no! Oh God, no! [It's alive!]

41

Look, Mada. Tomorrow is going to be the last day
of my stay here – and still I haven't found out
who it is lives right over there just across the landing! –
though certainly I'm still at least *mildly* interested.
(And there's surely still time enough to do so, is there not?)

42

Unable to sleep in an unfamiliar room,
I pick up an anthology of [great but] very poor poetry
from all round the world – written by men and women
who, without exception, did at least manage successfully
to die a reassuringly lengthy amount of time ago.

43
"Of course, there always remains the distant past
to come to terms with, Aeve – but are we not aided here
by a deep down sense, at some very basic level, out of which
we may even [in part?] be built, that, even at their liveliest and best,
they were never *quite* as real as we so effortlessly are now? Yes?"

44
"Ah, if this wonderful, fine, cool morning light,
is not, say, like a much-welcome vintage trickling down
over the charming, fresh buttocks of an amenable young goddess –
then it is indeed hard to decide just what it *is* like, Eve.
What else could it be? Let's see. Hmm. Not her mother, surely?"

[Which reminds me of one of my own poems, in fact. To wit: "In the
supermarket, at first / I thought this particular packaging / was showing the
nice full plump buttocks of a sinuous rococo nymph – / however, on
investigating more closely, I found instead / it was in fact an *Indian Cuisine
Gourmet Snack Selection*."]

45
Oh, God, God – how could I have been so stupid
as to help produce children out of
that extremely strange and alien woman?
I thought to myself –
before at once realising, Niamh, to my immense relief –

46
Then I woke up right beside her arms
from a dream which definitely featured one of her arms
in it somewhere –
My God! What a world! I thought.
(Oh, if only they could now find *Love's Labour's Won* too!)

[Routinely considered to be a lost early play of Shakespeare, presumably
brilliant. (When you think what *rubbish* can survive!)]

47

What else was I expected to do?
There was something else I had been asked to do,
wasn't there? Yes. All the way back
I am trying to remember. Searching for the keys
in various pockets, I am still trying to remember.

48

That minute or so just before
I saw her for the first time!
It's gone, of course.
Completely gone. Annihilated. Yes.
But somehow I have more or less survived myself.

49

Oh, I never expected
to see a golden snake
glide across
our kitchen floor
quite like that, my darling!

50

Yes, Eve. My mother once told me
she tried to get rid of me as a child –
but at the time, I assumed
she could only be exaggerating for (you know?)
crude melodramatic effect.

[And things that find it intolerable (a rare phenomenon?) presumably must
inevitably change into other things which have no such qualification?]

51

"I'm sorry, Dante. I realise
one shouldn't say this, of course –
but the simple fact is that other people's sufferings
were unquestionably far inferior to my own. Yes. In fact,
they have something unquestionably a little comic about them, I'm
    afraid. Sorry."

[I'm not sure that this is much – if indeed any – of an improvement on the
original version: "Really, Dan – who is much interested / in other people's
sufferings? – / particularly when they can have the chance / of listening to
me [or even you?] / talk about the real thing?"]

52

No, Eve – and I never expected
to see a second snake
glide sinuously across
my kitchen floor
quite like that either!

53

Oh, look! An escaped plastic bag
is blowing through the locked park over there
in the early morning. (Meaning?)
And who else, apart from the two of us,
[notices] is aware of it? (No one? Oh, no-one, I do so hope!)

54

(Oh, someone else did, my darling, I dare say.
By now I have found that someone else
nearly always does. Not invariably, true.
But we know we are really Adam and Eve.
And they – damn them! – know they are really Adam and Eve too.)

55

Look! Up there, among the leaves
of the neighbouring garden to ours!
Is that yet another living thing –
or the shadow of a living thing –
hmm – or maybe nothing much at all?

[It was a squirrel, actually. Though perhaps I shouldn't let the cat out of the
bag like that, Your Ladyship! (Eh?)]

56

Do you remember how once, Eve,
we stayed out in the garden more or less all night?
Why exactly were we doing that? Can you tell now?
Not for some mere technical *reason*, I hope?
Stars. Words. Warmth. What else? Because that too was possible?

57

Having, it seemed, accidentally locked ourselves out,
we sat down beside a politely decomposing wall,
slipped through a gap in the fabric of the universe –
or so I now tend to assume – and quite disappeared. Nobody
noticed our mutual absence for at least another hour or so.

58

Just outside Edinburgh, I saw from the passing train
a detached house-door – propped up against a garden wall!
I kept my eye on it for as long as I could.
But – (alas)
no-one ever quite saw fit to emerge from it.

59

New Year's Day. Hanging up yet another calendar,
I find – at long last! – I am using the final one
from that little box of drawing-pins which I bought – (why?) –
in a none too distant city which I have not been back to
in surely rather over a decade ago by now? [Aberdeen.]

60

What? Did you – eh? What? Did I really see that
just there on the packed train drawing out of Lenzie?
A huge man carrying a detached car door down a lane?
And yet – why shouldn't I have done? Only last week,
I saw a large fox from the train window, did I not? [Perhaps.]

61

'The train halts routinely at the nondescript station.
A few more heads are thrown out of it.
Then it trundles nonchalantly on to the next stop.'
(Hmm. I think I must have jotted this down years ago.
Something I read, perhaps? Or is it merely from me?)

[Well, at the very least, a fairly accurate description of certain aspects of
life.]

62

Such interesting snippets of conversation
one hears on the train these days
(thanks to the mobile phone) –
"Oh, him! He died late last year.
Yes. Yes. I know the feeling all too well!"

63

All day, such appalling rain! Somehow
caught in the house, a wasp is now carefully investigating
and investigating the top folds of the lace curtains at the window.
After a while, I lose patience, get up from my seat, go over, trap it
and squash it. Then I stand for a while looking out of the window.

[There you are. Real death. One up from so many epics. Odd, all the
same, that removing a single insect out of the billions of them flickering
through the Universe past and present should make one feel *quite* so guilty.
Thank God it at least didn't say much before it left. (Almost certainly
nothing, in fact.) Surely that would have made things so much worse?]

64

Later, as we wandered almost idyllically through the gentle city park –
I, alas, found my enchanted state increasingly compromised
by the desperate need for a certain type of crude physical relief.
      However,
at roughly this point there was a loud bang – and I (perhaps even
both of us?) disappeared! Yes. So it all worked out pretty well in
            the end, didn't it, darling?

65

All these more or less sexual parts in the glorious flowers
which are flaunted nearly all over this newly established country! –
variously inside – (or just outside) – so many admirable houses –
lovely! Democracy, eh? (Or whatever it is!) What next?
But who exactly, Eve, buys all this entrancing food [or underwear]?

66

"You know, I think I might quite like to die
while eating a very slightly unripe banana
in the understanding presence of
an angel – always, of course, assuming
it was female, and had nice big feathery wings."

[A close thing, one feels.]

67

(Why do I talk
as if angels are female?
Well, I don't really know. Isn't it
just kind of *obvious*
that angels are female? No?)

68

As we wandered idyllically through the gentle city park,
alas, I had to climb [up] down smartly behind some thick bushes
and relieve myself like a clap of thunder. When I at length returned,
she had [perhaps not so] mysteriously disappeared
and a large nude angel was waiting there for me with an even
        larger [penis] frown.

69

You know, Adan, I do so love to catch a thrilling glimpse
of one of my wife's delicate pieces of technical construction
while she tells me a little more of the unknown streets and rooms
in which, according to her, she used to live for a while –
and completely enough, it would seem – long before she met me.

[It's a deliberate misprint. (So much of the best writing is.)]

70

"Yes, indeed. Let me presently stop talking
of what does not really interest me all that much –
and instead henceforward confine myself,
O my incomparable Amedea, to what does.
Yes. Oh, and to poetry too, I suppose. Why not?"

71

"For the fact is, Adam, if only my wife's various apertures
could be directly translated into literature,
it would turn out to be such a damn sight more interesting
than absolutely all the poetry and so forth together
that has ever been written anywhere near here. No?"

[Hmm. Probably not all that much of a compliment really. Though I dare
say a certain amount depends on just what 'here' means.]

72

"Yes, Madam, I am a poet. When at work,
I have deep thoughts about God, the sea, voles, shrubbery
and such-like. Occasionally I marvel
that other people pay me so curiously little attention.
Still, I am brave about this. Yes. Terribly, terribly brave."

73

"Oh! A fairly close relative of mine has just died, darling!
Not you – thank God! Still. At least there ought to be
a couple of decent poems in it, eh? (Hand me over my dictionary,
will you, there's a love!) And I'll be terribly *spontaneous*
about it too – God, yes, of course. (People will just *love* me for that!)"

74

Again unable to sleep, for some reason or other,
I pick up a none too slim anthology of esteemed poetry –
and, never entirely certain that I'm still awake,
I read through it more or less to the end.
And to think I could have been unconscious all this time!

75

In my dreams, I so often
venture very profitably south of the river,
I am hard put to understand
why it never so much as crosses my mind to go there
for years on end, during my waking hours.

76

The last time I was in this fairly narrow street
(several weeks ago now, I think)
I saw something in it which struck me immensely.
But what the hell was it? No. I can remember –
only that something struck me immensely round about here.

77

Every night the same thing happens –
but what does it matter?
Morning comes along in any case!
And if some day it doesn't –
well then. The darkness will just have to do instead.

78

Morning. It's raining heavily again!
But can I really still be here
and still be alive? (Apparently.
Yes.) And can the new carpets still be here too –
as beautiful as they were yesterday? (Yes! Yes!)

79

"Well, Vi(e), at least, I suppose,
I don't have to worry
about disappointing anybody.
And anyway, how could I possibly
have had the success I deserve?"

80

"Yet, you know, occasionally
I feel I must be breaking some sort of world record
for personal failure, the Lord remarked to me once,
Fourth Dan – but I dare say we *all*
must feel like that at times, don't we?"

81

Yes! It's 10.42
and I still have an absolutely enormous vital part!
Isn't life just so wonderful, Breve?
And now it's 10.43! Yes! The whole damn thing
just seems to go on and on forever, doesn't it?

82
Heaven? Yes! Those buses, for instance!
These street details! And what, Sir, may I ask,
is that quasi-phallic object over there? Oh, I see. Yes.
Well, I've never been a *particularly*
religious person myself, I must admit.

83
Are you talking about
what I think you're talking about?
Because, listen, Beatrice – if you are –
if you are – though, actually, the main thing
was nearly always the need for more money –

84
"Oh, it just kept telling me
that really nonetheless in some sense
I am – or we are, darling – much better off
than they are – or, indeed,
than it is. Yes. So. What are you thinking, Adam?"

85
"These angels here? Huh. Absolutely useless,
I would say. The most you can reasonably
ask for is that they don't harm you – rather than that
they might be any good at their job. You know, quite frankly,
in my opinion, Dantai, all the best ones got out."

86
"Nothing has recently entered
this nondescript old municipal pond
as far as I'm aware, O Son of Mangodna –
except perhaps for a gigantic detached goat's head
which fell right out of the dark sky at midnight."

87
What's this? Empty space!
Yes, Pan! Completely empty!
Except, I suppose, for a few billion
love-letters floating about in it.
Yes! Yes, look! That one there's possibly [yours] mine!

88
"You know, darling, I wonder whether *any*
of my new neighbours here realise –
or are even remotely interested in the fact –
that they have a potentially
world-shattering genius in their midst?"

89
He whose underpants
start to talk [wisely] to him
is certainly right to be concerned, Berenice.
And at least equally concerned should be he
who finds himself sitting next to him on, say, the local bus.

90
Such interesting snippets of conversation
one hears on the train these days
(thanks to the mobile phone) –
"Oh well, you had to do your best.
Perhaps I was never really alive to begin with, darling."

[Indeed, sometimes the change may be effected within a single head!]

91
That chap sitting beside me on the airport bus
certainly seemed to be carrying a[shocked-looking]n extra head –
but I decided after all not to interfere.
I'm not his judge. Besides which, one can so easily
imagine doing something exactly like that oneself. No?

[Many variants exist. For instance: The chap beside me / on the bus /
seemed to be carrying / a [shocked-looking] severed head – but, ever /
considerate, I thoughtfully looked away. Or: (– but no: I felt / it wasn't
quite my place to interfere.) Or, after a two-line opening, perhaps on
another form of transport: (but, hey! Live and let live! / Just let them
respect my privacy – / and I'll quite happily respect theirs!) And: (discon-
certing at first, of course – / but why should I interfere? That's / what the
staff are paid for, is it not?) Etc. etc.]

92
Such interesting snippets of conversation
one manages to overhear on the train these days
thanks to the mobile phone:
"Oh, I do so agree with you!
Yes. I do *so* agree with you!"

93
"Also, it is quite important, Master,
for you to live at least as long as you can –
if only to show – ('But am I not in Heaven?') –
that people who think as you do
are not necessarily thereby driven to top themselves. What's that?"

94
"Well, anyway, where would I ever have got to, Damnte,
without, you know, my late wife's magnificent bust – er, bequest?
Quite apart from the utterly astonishing rest of her! Eh?"
("But, Sir, I'm afraid – erm – I'm afraid that, just at present, you're
    in Hell.")
"Am I? Shit! Is this Hell? God! You know, I do wish you hadn't
    told me that."

95

("Oh, dear God! You know,
I do so rather wish
you hadn't told us that. Talk about
depressing all and sundry with
an excess of information!")

96

The most important thing, I think,
that life has taught me, darling,
is that other people
are to some extent unique and matchless exfoliations
of the effectively infinite subtleties inherent within material
        possibility. ["What's that, dear?"]

97

It seems, Undan, she might have accepted
the Great Man (who adored her) as a lover –
had it not been for the fact
that she found him physically repulsive – and, besides,
(as it now turns out), she already had a lover at the time.

98

("I'm sorry, darling. But the fact is: I just find you,
if we're to be quite honest, physically repellent –
(and honesty is so important between us two, isn't it?) –
besides which, I, erm, I already – erm – well, in fact,
I already have a lover at the present time. Okay?")

99

"Darling, I do so very much hope
that what I fear to be the case
is not in fact the case –
however, if it is,
then that is the end of that, all right?"

100
They talk of love, and so forth.
Well, yes – I do so myself, Circe.
But, alas, does any emotion
play a much greater part in our lives
than sheer, unconquerable self-delusion?

[Almost certainly yes, since you ask.]

101
"Huh. If life is a
disappointment, darling, then just think
what *death* is going to be like!
(Oh God, no, Odysseus –
I'm doing it myself now!)"

102
"Oh God, yes!
How I must have idealised him or her!
You know, for a while,
I even thought he or she was almost
half as real or intelligent as I am myself!"

[Ridiculous, I know, eh?]

103
"Of course, one does what one can,
Mary, within the actual limitations
of the reality around oneself –
which, in my particular case, are pretty huge.
As, for that matter, fortunately, is my necessary equipment."

104
"Oh, not me, Dan – I've never really understood
what life is. For a long while, yes, I tried to –
but it's easily defeated me. And so, these days,
basically – well, now I just try to grasp and penetrate
everything helpful that comes into my reach. And you?"

105
"Me? Oh, I rather glory,"
the huge angel said with a smile,
"in the ultimate utter
pointlessness of it all.
Don't you? No? Not really?"

106
What? Did you *really* not say:
"Life would be quite unbearable
if it were actually happening?"
No? Oh, my sincere apologies! I thought that
was what you said just then. I'll let you go at once.

107
"Damn! It looks increasingly
as if we might have fallen, Adam,
right into the trap
which non-Existence itself has,
with such a rare slyness, created for us!"

108
"What, Dans? But there shouldn't be *any* children
in here now. You are quite sure you heard them?
How on earth did they manage to get through
the inviolable gates? Even the *bad* angels
couldn't quite manage that. Um. Excuse me a moment, wilt thou?"

109

You know, it must be the first day of another school year.
Listen. Once again that assembly bell is calling in
yet more loud new children to the school across from her flat.
Hm. But if our world really is the sound of a bell, O Master,
then what would you say – do tell us – is in fact the bell itself?

[Some advanced nonsense he was reading at the time, I suppose?]

110

And, darling, all those former children who used to play
in that now built-over park beyond the trees
must surely be wild-scattered to so many somewhere-elses –
all wondering – nearly all? – in his (or her) adult head:
Hmm. Just what the hell then is *actually going on here*? Eh?

111

What? My father a mere child
loitering on his way to school?
It's quite unthinkable! All those other
great swirling crowds of vanished children
are bad enough. (Get a move on, Dad!)

112

"To be quite honest about it, darling –
no offence – but I think I rather preferred
that dazzling free life I feel we must have had
before any of these f★★★ing priceless children of ours
happened to come along. Erm. No. Only joking, of course."

113
You know, Eve, there are times
when for a moment I cannot quite tell
whether these screaming sounds come from the children
down there or the [angels] seagulls up there. What do the insects
make of it all, do you think? But – absolutely nothing, I dare say.

["Really, darling? And what do the insects *ever* make of it all?"]

114
"To neither, of course, of my German grandparents –
whose names I could tell you – did the bare thought even occur –
how could it have done, darling? – that my father might meet
        someone
in an improbable foreign country, and there help produce
strange, alien children whom they would never even learn of."

115
All these variously loved children
speaking their strange languages, Adam –
by now I feel I may have had enough!
How I wish sometimes the ancient ocean
had known just a little less. Is that permissible?

[Or: "All these loved children / speaking their strange languages – / I have
had enough! / I wish the ancient ocean / had known just a little less."]

116
No, Dun(e). Something has gone
very badly wrong here.
Was water perhaps supposed to cover
the whole planet? No? No?
But just look how near [to that] it got!

117

"You know, it always rather astonishes me, Fa-ling,
that our small native country
is actually discernable at all
even upon a sufficiently large
globe of the world, such as this one here."

118

"Er, well, I have come up here
to your extremely beautiful country –
well, basically, in order to die, I suppose. Yes.
I hope you don't mind – do you? No, it's something
I've been meaning to do off and on for quite a long time."

119

Well, Eve, when anyone ever asks me
if I feel that Death is inhuman –
or something roughly like that –
I usually just reply, "No."
(Or something roughly like that.)

120

But for me, darling, almost invariably
part of the experience of listening
to such gorgeous, time-suspending music
is the thought of: "Please, let it go on! Let it not stop yet!" –
which is in itself of course a sense of time continuing to pass.

121

Perhaps the best performances
are those which somehow vaguely remind one
of what the real music should ideally be like?
Or is that perhaps a bit too much like life itself?
Hmm. (And then again, Eve – what isn't?)

122
Why have I pinned
that picture of an atomic explosion
above my narrow, chaste bed?
Oh, to remind me of the good times,
darling, I suppose.

[I suspect, if this had been one of mine, I would probably have been
tempted to finish it more along the lines of : Because I wish the females in
my life to doubt, if only for a moment at least, just who in the end is the
final boss here. On the other hand, I'm not quite sure that that would
sound acceptably ironic enough.]

123
I feel comparatively little desire, Odysseus,
to be a sudden unpredictable wave which perhaps runs over
a delightful young girl's recumbent body
as she lies (presumably) on a beach somewhere –
unless perhaps the shock causes her to whisper: "Life!"

[A somewhat different / four-letter word / from the one I had / antici-
pated, / I admit.]

124
"But that has been my whole life, has it not?
Thimblefuls judging the ocean, my Beatrice.
Not that that's really for me to say, of course.
With myself as the ocean, let me quietly add,
darling – to forestall any possible ambiguity."

125
"For, alas, so much of what
I can hardly quite say in public
seems to me, Eyes, to be
precisely the sort of thing that *someone*
ought to be saying in public. No?"

126
No. I'm afraid the Doors
of the Mausoleum[RrBur]
to the unusually Great Poet
are normally kept locked these days –
mainly, I am told, for understandable security reasons.

127
"Really? Is that really how it happens, Mother?
Was I not just sort of already waiting
somewhere upstairs? (I presume there was an upstairs?)
(And who, for that matter,
was right next door at the time?)"

128
"Oh, believe me. Thinking once again, Deirdre – er, Featrice –
of those absolutely disgusting scenes which I witnessed
while I was down there, I am intensely ashamed
of the extremely powerful feelings – er, Beatrice –
which somehow or other they managed to evoke in me."

129
And yet, S[a]tan, even these utterly horrible women
somehow can flickeringly remind me
of the kind of women I like. (Perhaps
it might have something to do with the fact
that they are all women? Yes. Yes. Might that not be it?)

130
"Although always, I think, Dan, in safe and certain possession of
some 97 out of the 100 major qualities which any
reasonable woman might conceivably need – yet somehow
I never really seemed to meet any woman who did not most need
precisely those missing three! So, Shitface. How do you explain *that*?"

131
Me? Oh, why ask me? I could compile
such a wonderful book of *Things Not To Say To Women*
merely by writing down with appropriate accuracy
all the stuff that happens to make its way into my poor head
more or less every second moment of every single day.

132
"Then one day, Dan, many years afterwards, from some
mildly irritated gesture she made, I suddenly –
to my astonishment – realised: maybe
she doesn't much like it
when I do [or say] things like that!"

133
"In my view, they are more or less all at it, darling.
I shall say nothing more about it.
No. Everywhere is my – what? – quite frankly, Adam –
I was hoping for a *little more respect*. I was. Yes.
Even if only from the bloody Universe as such."

134
It just doesn't look even remotely the same
without the girls here, does it, Dansei?
No. Just not remotely right.
We shouldn't have talked to them like that.
(Mind you. *What else* could we have honestly said?)

135
Of course (as God himself once
or twice said to me) really it's not at all
about trying to annoy people, is it?
No. After all – what, Beatrice,
would be the *point* of that? Absolutely none, dear.

136

No, dear, I am not trying to be
provocative. It's just – well, it's just –
well, I'm afraid I've just more or less ceased
to more or less give a flying (you know) f★★★
one way or the other, Berenice – er, Beatrice.

137

"Oh, if you only knew what a huge part of my life I have passed in
      thinking about you, Beatrice!" *(Liar! No, you haven't!)*
"Yes I have!" *(Turd! No, you f★★★ing well haven't!)*
"Yes I f★★★ing well have!" *(Then why didn't you kill yourself?)*
"What? Why – ?" *(And who the hell then is this Bernice?)*
"Darling, have you learnt f★★★ing NOTHING up here? Eh?"

[Apparently a touch of trouble and strife *in Paradiso*.]

138

("No. I don't much like
the sound of this, I'm afraid –
but it does seem
to be happening in Heaven,
for all that.")

[See?]

139

"Good morning, you utterly exquisite and ethereal creature!
So. Tell me honestly: what do you think of this here?
A rather impressive view, is it not, in the magical light of – oh, shit! –
wait a minute! Wrong way round! Yes! Okay. There we are.
Fine. Only my eldest son has one exactly like it, you know."

140

"Well, my opinion, Beatrice, since you ask for it is:
it would surely have already been quite enough
that women may be beautiful and have these haloes too.
But that we can also (at least at times) talk to each other!
My God, it's just too much, isn't it? Hello? Beatrice? Hello?"

["All beauty is female beauty." (Adams, I think?) (Wrongly, as it turns out.)]

141

Designed? How? With what real tools?
Better not to ask again, perhaps –
or have I got that
slightly the wrong way round? Hmm. I'm not sure.
Anyway – who [what bodiless substance] am I talking to now?

142

Oh, Dante – one just keeps seeing
the same people here over
and over again! – except of course
that we can't really see them
and they aren't really people –

[but, apart from that –]

143

"Have thou heard the latest, Adam?
It seems He's lately come up
with a third sex now as well!" "Oh,
it'll never catch on, Eve. No. Don't worry about it.
Still … erm … just, you know, as a matter of interest … "

144

Such interesting snippets of conversation
one hears on the public street in these advanced days
(thanks to the mobile phone) –
"Please just try to keep all three of them
as far apart as you can. All right?"

145

Maybe this God is something like
the dial-tone of the Universe, Adam?
But must you make that call? (I mean to say –
probably no-one will answer anyway.
You'll very likely only get a[n irritating] recorded message.)

146

Such a very cool response I got
when I rang you up last night!
And still a distinctly cool response
when I rang you up again this morning. Yes, Ove.
One is almost threatening to begin to understand.

147

Such interesting snippets of conversation one hears
on passing mobile phones these extremely advanced days –
"Well, why not go back and see?
No? – if it's *really*
worrying you all that much?"

148

No, but for a change of plan
I would in fact not be travelling
on the train this afternoon –
though, most likely, that voluble lawyer opposite me
would still be talking earnestly into his mobile phone.

149

All the more odd then that, several years later,
we should be talking to each other again like this!
Fairly easily, it seems – in fact, more or less
like normal reasonable adult human beings – (if there is
such a thing). (Which there is, of course, isn't there, Eve?)

150

"But we nearly all start out, Adam, do we not,
with grossly, later-embarrassingly, unreasonable hopes –
for aren't we yet unaware of more than the first whisper
of the hellish [heavenly] complexity even of this the simplest life
that seems to lie ahead?" ["Yes, Eve. True. So true. *Buttocks!*"]

151

yet works one's way thereafter, with so much [joyful] effort,
up to another ridge – surely this time the final one? –
only to see more and more extensively
an even greater everything
falling further and further away forever on all sides –

152

Huge faulty lights flash-
ing on and off in Heaven!
One might as well ex-
pect the light[n]ing itself to
care much about what we do!

153

"Oh, yes. Once I've be-
gun the work, I find I'm perf-
ectly all right. Yes.
Perfectly. It's starting it
that's the problem," said God to –

154
(Hmm. Well now, Adam.
How could *we* ever know
just exactly who it was He
was actually talking to? Eh?
Not his [Mother] Father, I trust?)

155
"No, of course I am not searching for a
'transcendental truth', Mum. And anyone
who *is* searching for some such thing is never in fact
going to find it anyway – the expression being a mere
contradiction in terms. No. Nice ham and eggs, by the way."

156
(There is only literal truth, Verity, isn't there?
No other real, unmetaphorical sort. No.
All truth is an expression of our own language
(or languages) in the more or less here and now.
(Just like untruth, in fact, now I come to think of it.)
[I could say more, but who else would particularly listen to me?])

157
"For not too many of you, I fear,
ever feel much compulsion
to pursue the Truth as such, O Oedipus. Rather,
you make up what you want to find
and this you call the [not to be questioned] truth."

158
Eh? Is that the final Truth, Eve,
hanging from those branches up there –
or are they merely more raindrops? Oh, yes,
darling – you're right! – it's actually an apple tree! Yes.
Yes. Yes. And just *look* at all those *lovely* apples!

159

"But does the Universe itself, I wonder, Eve, wonder
quite how my uniquely promising youth in fact slipped by?
It does seem rather unlikely, doesn't it? Hmm. Well, no.
No. Let's be even more honest here, shall we, darling?
It is in fact *extremely bloody* unlikely, is it not?" ["Yes, dear."]

160

Obviously, Adam, most of these people
who die fairly young
never really come close to understanding
just how little [more] of it all
they would ever have understood!

[Listen. Obviously, all these people who die fairly young never remotely
get to understand what trivial but real nonsense all this ageing business is.
(And so much else, for that matter!)]

161

And what if, as things happened, I hadn't cut through
that particular routine street, at that particular time?
Would we have met again later, do you think? (Or ever?)
What can I call it but a mere sudden impulse? Yes.
Mind you, isn't it nearly all a sort of sudden impulse?

[Yes. But if non-Existence hadn't succumbed to quite such a sudden, rash
impulse – oh my utter, lifelong beloved! – what then, what then, what
then, what then?]

162

"Oh, Adamk, if only we had had the chance,
the whole thing could have been otherwise – and so wonderful!
Or, indeed, so dreadful – yes – that I must concede too.
So different, at any rate. All these billions of moments
unlived among the leading of so many always flawed lives!"

163
Well, sometimes, Adam, yes, I doubt
whether any of this immortal work
is truly worth preserving – so, so much of it! –
but by now I sort of lack the energy
even to destroy it, you know?

[Perhaps the Deity speaking?]

164
"However, after a while,
[as for so many at least,]
it seems to be easier
to keep on doing it
than to stop doing it.
Or wouldn't you agree?"

165
So. I should just like to thank all those
who made it possible. And a particular thanks
to those of them who made it
more or less impossible. There, Beatresst.
Is that enough? (God, I very much hope so!)

166
(Or did *she* leave *me*?
You know, after a while, it gets
just so bloody difficult even
for someone as honest as myself
to remember *all* the bloody details.)

167
But it doesn't matter disproportionately much. No.
I might perhaps like to think it retained
some cosmic impossible significance – certainly
I used to do so – but, if it doesn't, my Beatrice,
then that too doesn't really matter much either, does it?

168

(Not that *anything else*
whatsoever, darling,
instead could in fact signify inherently
the least bit more. No. The same fabric,
after all, is [dispersed through] everything.)

169

And what else much anyway
does all this great truth of theirs amount to?
Apparently, that the incomparable Universe
is some sort of priceless coded message
sent by God to Himself!

['MEMO. Things to do. Must remember to create a Universe this time. Yes.
Don't forget again!']

170

"I don't know. Don't you think
we may perhaps be taking
unintelligibility
just a little bit too far,
Lord? (And I'm only asking!)"

171

But practically everything here
seems to be based on the [insane] premise
that someone somewhere is,
somehow or other,
going to somehow survive and somehow live forever.

[Yes, but how? In what actually real and conceivable way?]

172
And yet. obviously, I am
to some extent, darling, only
pretending to be
another person here
as well. (But please tell no-one.)

173
(That, Eve,
I should have thought
was obvious –
(perhaps too obvious?) –
to need stating!)

174
"No? Really? Well then, if you don't mind me asking,
what on earth is God going to do all day here? Eh?
Rather a chance missed there for the omniscient,
one might think, darling!" – ("Oh, please don't call me 'darling'.
It's *quite* the wrong place, and you don't *really* want me anyway.")

175
Yes, it terrifies me to think
what might be lurking in the small wood
just behind your house.
Not to mention
your strange and growing collection of [surely slightly dangerous?]
    shoes.

176
"No. I feel too much contempt
for this absolute shit-heap of a scarcely real world
to do it the undeserved honour, erm, Mary,
of being insuperably depressed
or, for that matter, remotely disappointed by it."

177

In fact, Marv, I sometimes wish I were a golden butterfly, wandering
over the scented landscapes of a good, kind, helpful woman
who had very little idea that I was actually there –
(Well, *neither* of us would have much of that, I suppose) –
or who, in fact, in some deep sense I even *was* really.

178

I am told, Elve, that the latest occupants
of that fine big house on the corner beside the bank
include a pair of almost absurdly beautiful
daughters. (Some say, three.) Hmm. They certainly
do own at least a couple of extremely impressive cars.

179

With only two or three days left
before I finally have to leave the place
where I've lived happily enough for several years now –
some unknown person rings me on the land-line
trying to contact some name I have never heard of.

180

That was such a very cool response I got
when I rang you up last night. And again
still such a noticeably cool response
when I rang you up again this morning. Yes. I know.
A lesser man might even have got the point by now.

181

Such interesting snippets of conversation
one hears on the train these days
(thanks to the mobile phone) –
"Don't give it another thought! (…)
I said – don't give it another thought."

182

Anyway, my angel, a few minutes ago I had an absolutely
fantastic idea for a long poem and how to organise it.
Do you by any chance want to hear it?
(No. Of course I don't.) Hm.
You're not really the man you once were, are you, Third Dan?

183

Publish this diary of mine
when I am dead, Eve, if you want to.
Or perhaps just destroy it instead? –
if that's the easier thing to do.
It hardly matters. Who'll miss it?

[He didn't really mean it!]

184

"Yes I did. Still: sudden, unanticipated extinction
is hardly much of a problem, is it, darling?
Darling? Eve? Hello? Eve? Are you asleep already?
For God's sake, woman! I'm making some really good
clarificatory points here! I mean to say. Why do I bother?"

185

And in the end, Adam,
nothing will save the All –
whatever else it is
it might have to be saved
from. (What could that be?)

186

And at once, for some reason,
a strangely reassuring thought
occurs to me, Adam.
Oh, no – wait a moment there!
It's just slipped away again!

187
Well, who else, Beatrice,
are you supposed to be?
What other colour, for instance, should white be?
The material laps this way – no? –
then laps that way, and then has always changed.

188
"Look. It's very simple. It's what they actually are.
Surely, Adam, if you really love them,
then the fact that all sorts
of complex physical stuff in fact comes out of them too
is simply something else you simply have to accept. No?"

189
Actually,
to be quite honest, Madam,
you are, I think, at best only the second person
who has ever commented even remotely favourably
on its extremely strange shape. So. Many thanks, dear, for that!

190
"You know, when at first admiring that impressive
row of sturdy, well-shaped objects
near the entrance to this great and deservedly celebrated shrine,
I did not at first realise, my darling,
that they in fact were fairly obsolete garbage receptacles."

[Jotted down at or near Benediktbeuern, I seem to recall.]

191
"Oh, it's a long story, Dangli. But, wishing to deflect attention
away from a trivial, hilarious and fleeting bout
of impotence – I (inadvertently, of course)
burnt down perhaps the oldest and most valuable (alas!)
of all the city's many great historic ecclesiastical erections."

[Obviously an inhabitant of one of the lower reaches is talking here.
Whereas, for instance, the question whether the subject of: "There he sits
all day / with his left foot / in his right hand / listening to the voice of God
/ emerging from his anus." is in Paradise, in Purgatory or in Hell is perhaps
slightly more difficult to decide than one might ideally wish. No?]

192
"For a long time, I confess, during my gloriously vanished youth
surely almost my greatest pleasure in life, before they blinded me,
lay in looking, Dant, at my girlfriend's leading erotic apertures
while she talked as nonchalantly as possible on the telephone
to one or other of her apparently innumerable relatives."

[Ditto?]

193
(I have noticed, Lord, that a certain element
of what you might call
anachronism
seems to creep in here every so often.
I take it it's deliberate?)

194
Only when nearly half-way through
listening to the new recording I had bought yesterday
did it suddenly occur to me
that the not unambiguously named soloist
might well not in fact be a man at all.

195
"Oh yes. It's a wonderful piece of music all right.
Time absolutely seems to stop, doesn't it?
In fact, Din(o), some performances
manage to make it last
for a full twenty minutes – possibly even more."

196
Again and again I hear from somewhere nearby
that same incessant, harsh, metallic
'cheep cheep cheep cheep cheep cheep cheep' –
What? Is this then all there is to be to it? For ever?
One noise, then another? Then another? Then another?

197
What? What was that? – someone sneezing
just outside, on the nearby street –
at midnight? A man, I suppose?
Going where? What? Why? [Were you asleep too?]
(Not something else in the room, I hope?)

198
I was sitting about in the converted attic
listening to a CD of some fifty-one different birdsongs
when I heard the main telephone begin to ring downstairs.
I ignored it. (Although whoever it was was calling
certainly took a long time to give the attempt up!)

[I was sitting working in the converted attic, Eave,
listening to a CD of some fifty different birdsongs
when I (only just) heard the phone ringing in the room below.
So. Do I make the effort to reach it or don't I?
(But it rang off *precisely* as I picked it up.)]

199
What's that? A piano upstairs?
No. I have never heard
a piano upstairs before.
And, you know – really, not
too badly played either!

200
Good Lord! Someone
is tuning a piano
right next door.
And I am just sitting here – am I not? –
nonchalantly listening to it!

201
Unusual silence at last from
one or other of the loud tree-sheltered gardens
not far across the summery lane.
I assume those noisy bloody children
for the moment at least are off being fed somewhere.

[This is obviously happening at the back of 226 Wilton Street – rather
than, say, anywhere in Wilson Street. (Though Wilson, as a matter of fact,
was that old couple's surname, wasn't it?)]

202
"What was that noise there, Adam?
Nothing? Hardly!
Did you not hear
something strange just then too?
From something slightly behind you, I think?"

203

"And just listen to that, my beloved Edem!
More squeaking and giggling coming somehow
from within yon glad little glade nearby!
You don't think perhaps this simple new superstition
might be a lot more fun than we had at first assumed?"

204

No, I haven't, Eve. No. Not yet.
Nor (I suspect) have you.
I mean to say, dear, if we had,
we'd probably both be
dead by now, wouldn't we, darling?

[Syllabics? 8.6.8.6.8. (But so what, *Maestro*?)]

205

"I too quite like the fact, Adam,
that it's now five minutes past five
on New Year's morning – and that therefore
we have both survived into another
real year. (Or have I missed something important?)"

206

and now another sunlit morning! – perfect! –
already nearly eight o'clock again –
so much beauty flickering even in this small room –
nobody (it seems) has harmed us lethally –
what next? – my infinite[ly] unended universe

207

But what is quite happening, O Lord?
My thoughtful wife is still wearing
nothing but her underwear –
even though it's now nearly
ten o'clock on a Sunday morning –

208
Turning the corner of a routine, pleasant street
on yet another Saturday morning
on my way to buy a few more normal but
needed items of food – (what keener bliss,
truly, Eve, have I ever known?) –

[A rather sheltered life? Chiefly decent bread and certain types of cheese, I
suppose. How I envy him! (By the way, surely it's not entirely without
interest that this was at one point followed by 196?)]

209
Well, I have sat here admiring your beautiful face
in this dull room more or less all morning.
There must be other things you have to do?
What? No? Oh, well.
All right then. Another coffee maybe?

[Oh, yes. Coffee too!
Though, actually, it was much more usually tea, was it not?]

210
12.12.12
on my old digital watch. My God!
When I last glanced at it –
I'm sure it said: *11.11.11.*
And how long, long ago was that?

[One for the more technical critics, obviously.]

211
"For me, Durante, the new celestial day
cannot even be said to have properly started
until I have had sex with someone
whose necessarily inferior intelligence I nonetheless genuinely
    admire.
(Yes. It can be a lonely life sometimes, I admit.)"

212
"I wonder if any
of my [angelic] neighbours even here
realise – or are at all interested in the fact –
that I too have potentially
not entirely inactive genitals, Dan?"

213
But we have to talk
about these things too, darling!
Otherwise,
what sort of a description
of any real life is it at all?

[Yes. It would be like *Romeo & Juliet* without Juliet – and, for that matter,
without Romeo too. (Not that I greatly like the play, I admit. (Compared,
say, to *Lola's Wonne*.))]

214
(Though nobody really knows
anything at all about
any of this,
do they? Except
me! [Me! Me! Me! Me!])

215
"Actually, Dan, the first indisputable sign I had
that the massively absurd argument might finally have expired
came when she suddenly leant over towards me
in the back of her mother's car and whispered: 'Hello there.
Of course you can —— me all night tonight, if you want to.'"

[A scene from *Purgatory*, I assume. I decline, however, to attempt to fill in
the illimitably mysterious gap. 'Indisputable' does rather seem to be the *mot
juste* here, doesn't it, Stevie?]

216
In a wild but rather delightful state of puzzlement,
Juliet at last lowers the latest love-sonnet
(received that very morning from Romeo) −
and turns to ask her Nurse: "Nurse? Nurse?
Tell me, Nurse. What exactly does 'squirt' mean?"

[A sad piece of presumably juvenile prurience, alas − which I have taken
the liberty of slightly cleaning up − chiefly in the interests, I suppose, if it's
quite the phrase, of the still not entirely exhausted language of heterosexual
enchantment. Other candidates for penultimate inclusion rush copiously
forward to suggest themselves − but, quite frankly, Bill, such endeavours
have long since begun to bore me.]

217
"Dan, I would still rather like to telephone someone (possibly
a young nun?) and discuss with her some of the subtler differences
between right and wrong. (Perhaps a nurse?) Or, failing that −
have we had another argument? − listen to her seductively
whisper "I still have a c——!" before putting the phone down."

[Ditto, in effect.]

218
Such interesting snippets of one-sided conversation
one hears on the street these days
thanks to the mobile phone −
"Oh, of course it's not quite the right word!
It never bloody is, is it? Not for you."

219
"Well, Odom, one thing
I *have* found out thus far
is that very few women
seem to appreciate being told that −
or is it perhaps just how I say it? − "

220
But what's this on the bedside table?
I must have jotted it down
on the pad there during the night:
What? What the f*** do you mean:
'[Evidently] essentially incomplete'?

221
"What do I mean by that, Eve?
I mean exactly what I say!
Who here has not noticed something like this?
A certain elusiveness
about it all? What? Oh, yes, yes.

222
"What – only once – all this battery of learning and mistakes –
to be right at once and only once – no second chance –
therefore there must surely be a second performance –
learned from, this wisdom put to use – how we think –
or at least some sort of judgement – possibly some well-earned
    applause –

223
"Or else is all this wisdom *not* to be put to use?
(to do what? for it must all come
if from elsewhere from greater wisdom anyway –
therefore in itself quite superfluous –
additional, quite unnecessary, is it not? – or everything

224
"Oh yes. Gabrielli. I well remember the day
when I first felt I fully understood it all.
Yes. It felt just great. Yes. Wheee!
It felt just great to feel I fully understood it.
Yes. Just great. I mean, *really* great, you know?"

[Surely not God? And certainly not the *Trinity*!]

225
"I think you'll find, darling, I have never
claimed to be particularly open
to the achievements of other civilisations
and cultures, if any. And whose exactly *is* this God
who is punishing us all in here, by the way? And why?"

226
"Indeed, indeed.
I am miles beyond you all, I fear –
although quite possibly
away down yet another wrong road,
I have to freely admit."

227
Well, I tried hard not quite to
love her – I suppose – but, as it happens,
I failed. (If you could call that a failure.
(Oh, it was failure all right, darling!
(And did you *really* try anyway?)))

228
"That some people you meet so casually, [First] Dann –
in the wrong office, say – whom it seemed
that you just as easily (perhaps even more easily)
might never have risked talking to – should soon
turn into so much of what continuing life depends on!"

[Yes, yes. It's the wrong universe entirely – even if it's the only possible
one. (Or perhaps especially if!)]

229
Or did I choose the wrong one
ultimately, darling? Is this perhaps the wrong flat?
Which is the nearest star? Not that one, surely!
All right. [Do these new spectacles really suit me?]
Very well then. Which is the second-nearest star?

230
So. Have you too seen
the bus station at Parktic?
The trees? The warm wall
of a matchless invisible castle
where the right hand beckons from a window?

231
or those dreadful high-rise flats not too far away –
maybe being sick in one of the lifts late at night –
or, perhaps, the very next morning, Odysseus,
groping some gullible female in the same one –
sometimes even just travelling up and down, I suppose –

[Lifes? Lifts?]

232
"Oh, look! People!" she said –
crossing the room with quick and elegant steps
to have a look at a photograph on the wall –
in fact, of my now dead mother, smiling tentatively
as she stands waiting at a bus-stop in Switzerland.

233
"You know, I've never seen *anyone*
using those short-cut stairs in my *entire*
life," she remarked, leaning out
a little further from the usually closed front-room
window. (And it showed off her backside a bit more.)

[Surely a somewhat unfortunate juxtaposition, Athol? I mean to say, this
can hardly be someone's now dead mother, can it? (Idiot! Surely it's the
woman who elegantly crossed the room? (After all, a mother is hardly a
particular human rarity – is she, San? Crash!))]

234

"Oh, I never hear *anything* in this bloody place.
I never *see* anything in this bloody place
either. What do you think
can be going on right now, for instance,
in that bloody boring-looking golden mansion over there?"

235

"Oh, not only do you have to work out for yourself
so much of this easily missable artistic nuance stuff –
you also have to somehow manufacture a path through
the utter rubbish forever being thrown out in your way
by the rich shoals of salaried halfwits all around you."

236

Tell me: has anyone ever jotted down a poem
in this little kitchen before now, do you think? Eh? Never?
Not that you're aware of? Yes! That'll do for me!
(On the other hand, how much – even right here –
is one ever, Eve, quite unquestionably aware of?)

237

"For me to do exactly the same thing
decades later! – it's so ridiculous! Me! –
who still contains such numerous memories
of what turns out to be – can it be? –
dear God, the ground-away 1950s already!"

238

"For instance, Ive, I remember how, forty-odd years ago,
my late father once got stopped for [very slightly] speeding
while giving me a lift to school (unprecedented!)
hurriedly through drab but adequate streets which now
are hardly (why?) still there any more. (Trivial, I know!)

239

And not until several days after arriving there
do I finally get round to lining up once again
on a very sheltered bookshelf in my new room –
a clutch of by now utterly indispensable pictures
of a few lovely faces. (Yes indeed, dear. And what else?)

240

Can there be any more than a single part
of all the subtle and wide-ranging beauty
of this exquisite country of ours
that I want to be truly close to this morning, my Eve! –
and, wonderfully, there you are just there beside me!

241

"Well, in fact she had
tiny breasts and, if anything,
an even wobblier – er, smaller
sense of history – but I
still liked her a very great deal, Da, I must say."

242

But just how close did they ever get to each other?
The same airport? The same train?
The same street?
The same building? Oh God!
I'm amazed sometimes I even dare to look round!

[You know, I'm sure it was *** ****** ******* I saw recently in my
dreams. He was standing outside a building marked: C**** *Only Library* –
apoplectic, looking for volunteers to help him storm this 'f***ing disgrace
to our non-existent f***ing democracy'. I thoughtfully pointed out that
the sign as it stood was am-f***ing-biguous. How we laughed! Or turned,
as desired, into Dance, Edam and Allegorical Doughnuts. Or whatever it
was. (Or am I merely talking about *myself* again?) (Sometimes one simply
loses track of the whole ridiculously complex business, does one not? (But
don't just take *my* word for it, NhEaVE!))]

243
Walking back to the flat again
after another visit to the nearby library,
I stop for a few moments, struck by the sight
of a dignified elderly gentleman, off in the distance,
doing his laborious best to get down from a high wall.

244
I suppose I should have spent more time
in all the various palaces while I was there.
But somehow just getting on and off
their neat, clean, never-long-to-wait-for buses
always seemed to be pretty much enough for a real life.

245
"You know, darling – isn't it round about here
that that weird grandmother of yours used to live?
Or am I maybe thinking –
as I so often am these days –
of someone else entirely? (Which the Good Lord forbid!)"

246
"So please don't throw an old fool over completely
for these young things – no – they can't offer you
even a *tenth* of what I can offer you, darling.
And I'm not just talking about money either!
Though, as you know, Adam, I *do* have quite a bit of money."

247
On the other hand, darling,
I have to admit
it is almost the last thing
I would ever want to try
to bring myself to imagine.

248
Such at least
is my disgraceful plan.
No? Oh, all right then.
No. No – by all means watch
a bit more television first. (Good God!)

249
I am told that
last night
after –
erm –
all those interacting triple-stars, eh?

250
Still clutching the dim,
newly-found child to her chest,
she slowly crouched down
among the bright flowers and
disappeared into the earth.

[Persephone?]

251
"I want to go back there!
Keep the palaces for yourselves
by all means, ye Sons of Glengap!
A sort of fish? Who? Me?
Oh, no. I hardly think so!"

[Or even something Pictish after all?]

252
"But do not let them bury me
separate from my head,
O Captu Son of Kapttu.
Though I accept as yet it probably
makes no difference *technically*."

[No? Then what on earth is going on here?]

253
"Standing in the park,
Scaird, watching three crows wrangle
I suddenly felt
my head, arms and legs fall off
and roll away into town."

[Kindly get back to the bloody point, will you?]

254
Not quite at this park-bench here –
not quite the noise of that present traffic –
thoughts from another, similar moment
begin to threaten to invade me.
I drag the dog off into forward movement again.

255
"But perhaps it has
something to do with the fact
that we no longer
say too much to each other.
Might that not be it, Adam?"

256

Yes, Beave, you're right. it is high time for me
to buy a new dictionary. That much is self-evident.
By now, I've completely worn the old one out.
(Though rarely, alas, by quite managing to find
whatever it was I happened to be looking for.)

257

But what has gone amiss, my darlings,
with all those sundry gorgeous communications
I so much wanted to receive?
Did someone else get them, do you think?
And yet, how many ever do? (Did you?)

258

No, darling. No, that can't have happened!
It simply can't have happened.
I'm telling you. It simply can't have happened.
I have absolutely no desire to close my eyes to an unwelcome truth.
I'm simply telling you, Eve. It can't have happened.

[A routine response to *The Fall of Man*, I dare say. (Mind you – if that's
what he's talking about then it *didn't* happen.]

259

"The years continually drift past – Odysseus.
I get old, I suppose. From time to time
a goodish woman still opens her heart to me.
Indeed. Quite that. Nothing much else ever happens.
No. In fact, pretty much perfect, I should say."

260
"For almost three years now, I
haven't stepped inside that shop
next door to the bank —
though presumably, Elle, it would still be
as welcoming to me as ever?"

261
"Oh yes, I dare say
it might just be possible
to risk going in there again
some time quite soon,
Adam, erm, darling."

262
"Because, Elle,
to be brutally honest,
I still don't really know
whether I can trust myself to
again yet or not. Is that all right?"

263
Well, is it what you want?
Or is it what you *don't* want?
Or is it both?
Or is it neither? —
my silent but complex favourite! —

264
And what am I doing,
wandering around this house alive
now that she is dead? (But who is dead?
No, I never had a single clue
all my bloody life.)

[Which is to say, I think, that no one is actually dead. Which is to say, that
Death is not (somehow! the eternal somehow!) a state of being. That Non-
existence is not, as it were, a particularly subtle variety of Existence. Not a
roughly comparable variation of it. Death is a way of misconceiving that
which was once alive.]

265
And you go wherever
the encouragement is –
which is to say,
in my case at least, pretty much
nowhere. ("Oh, for God's sake, Adam!")

266
Maybe I should have been you
long long ago –
or does that make any sense?
On second thoughts, no.
It doesn't, does it, Eve?

267,
No. My thanks to all
who have allowed me to go on like this,
more or less unimpeded by the exquisite
vulgarities of success. And probably even of failure.
(Oh, Adam! For God's sake! Will you please stop doing that!)

268

But was that not success in life
already? If not, Master, then what
would worldly success ever really have been like?
Well? Perhaps if she had kept her clothes off
for the entire bloody week? Would that have done it?

269

"Oh, I would hardly have thought it possible
to fail quite so heroically
as just at present I do rather seem to have done –
but I dare say I probably flatter myself, Dante –
like more or less everyone else – men included."

[Quite a lot seems to depend by what exactly is meant by 'men' here, I
suppose?]

270

Oh, I have had absolutely everything –
except perhaps worldly success!
And, even there, Lord,
is there not a fairly general agreement
that worldly success is not really worth having?

[I don't know – but for quite a long time now it has somehow been
becoming more and more obvious to me that the Universe itself is essen-
tially a bit of a failure – and that human beings are very likely one of its few
successes. (Perhaps, indeed, its only real success?)]

271

" – insects which, for instance, darling,
say, explode in mid-air
when they just happen to grasp
the concept of death –
what? you mean then, I'm not – "

272
Dan, the flea
bites Leonardo – if it does, darling –
as merely one more part
of the eternal food chain – though 'eternal'
is (as usual) not quite the word, is it, Adam?

273
"No. With every passing year, Dan,
I find one appreciates ever more greatly
one's own complete personal unimportance.
But then, without something like that,
I dare say it wouldn't really be Heaven at all, would it?"

274
Coming down from the summit
after a wonderful hour or so alone
with peace, distance and light – he lost his footing
and, suddenly plummeting, almost at once
became a mere physical object again.

[Maybe much – or indeed all – of this is by way of being an epitaph, I
suppose?]

275
"You know, or a while, Virgil, I had almost
begun to doubt whether
she could even write at all –
until she started sending me
all those bloody suicide notes! – "

276
"Oh, Beatrice, God or not, I have crushed to death
very few entities, I am sure –
and all of them, my dear creature,
were *much* smaller than you or I. Yes. Much, much smaller.
Yes. Well. *Almost* all of them, certainly. Excuse me a moment, will
    you?"

277

It is, is it not, Beatrice, quite useless to deny
that little seems to impress
perhaps the vast bulk of us yet here
quite so much as do these wisps and wraiths
which don't even (which even *can't*) exist.

278

"How much truth
is there in it?" Hmm.
Well, for a start, Eve:
How much *possibility*
is there in it?

279

Do not say
that the entire visible universe
is only partly a sort of
metaphorical water-closet for the gods
or we'll batter your loved ones to death for it, all right?

280

"Oh God, yes, there must be toilets somewhere,
I would guess, in absolutely all of the
great religious buildings –
even if only hidden behind the scenes. Well.
Can't have the mere mortals using them, can we?"

281

Believe me, Penelope, it is certainly "no fun"
to be found hidden under one's own f***ing hallway floorboards
nearly some hundred and forty-seven years afterwards!
Couldn't you at least have looked there a little earlier, my dear?
Apart from anything else, I'm absolutely desperate for a piss!

[This certainly does not seem to fit any scene from one of the more canon-
ical versions of *The Odyssey*.]

282
Inside the little Garnethill tenement flat,
Eve suddenly crouched down for a gross spiritual
purgation – and, much to everyone's surprise,
out came [a cuckoo clock?] another world! How all the Gods
laughed [for a shimmering moment anyway]!

[This is, I am told, the oldest stratum of the present work, and therefore,
for reasons of historical accuracy, I retain it in all its appalling crudity. Of
course, it's hardly surprising that people deny the reality of death, when
they are so reluctant even to acknowledge the fact that they keep having to
shit. Indeed, most great spiritual leaders, questers, pursuers of the Ideal,
politicians[, angels] etc. would deny the fact completely if they thought
they could get away with it. But I dare say I labour here unnecessarily at an
extremely obvious point. (It is very noticeable, by the way, how often
commentators on Dante seem to talk as if he really might have been to all
these bizarre places he keeps burbling on about!)]

283
That chap down there has been carrying a ladder
to and fro opposite about the street all morning!
Who is he, Eve? – perhaps a valuable angelic Something?
Well, I mean to say, darling, we hardly ever
get much chance to see them here otherwise, do we? Yes?

284
Alas, thanks to one of these inevitable technical glitches
that slip in everywhere, the spirit arrived at the house
just when the Eternal Female had nipped out for a quick ——.
"Hello? What is it?" she shouted. "Erm. A fairly important
     announcement!"
it yelled back. "But don't worry. I'll wait. Yes, yes. I'll wait."

285

"Oh, it's such a strange business, isn't it, dear? As for my own
    beloved father –
he told me once he doubted if he had ever
felt fully aroused sexually – thus far at least –
even a dozen times in his entire life. (And – oh! – but I do so
    much regret now
that I failed to risk asking the screamingly obvious follow-up
    question!)"

286

So. What say you?
No?
No? Really?
Oh, all right then, darling.
Let's just forget it for now.

287

"But tell me, Adam: do these bizarre people who suppose
they must or might well be the only people who really exist
ever have sex with other people? Or with each other? If so,
what do they think is happening? Though, mind you, darling –
what is ever actually happening, even with the rest of us? Eh?"

288

"And what else then is the all up there –
oh my distinguished visitor! – but a single insect
more or less laying innumerable eggs
slightly beyond time and place
and without quite being alive? Oh, do pray tell me."

[This, rather obviously to my mind, is Satan speaking.]

289

"Is that [a plastic bag] a gigantic angel
hovering about some branches away over there
at the park gates?" "Yes! Yes, it is, darling! Why –
Oh no – wait a moment. On closer inspection –
No. No, it isn't, darling."

290

"Some shrewd remnant of my sense of human social tact,
O Dark Master, prevents me from too exactly describing
what happened (disastrously) next. Let me merely say –
this. This.
No. No. On second thoughts, I don't think I'll bother even with
    that. Sorry."

291

"Yes. Yes, I suppose you could say my life has been
more or less a disaster, O My Divine Visitor,
more or less all the way through.
Dear me. And yet, all in all, how extremely
fortunate I have been, compared to all these – well – all these –
    erm – "

292

Oh yes. If this world of his had been
a fairer place – yes. But it isn't. I mean,
why bother going on? Eh?
It isn't, Dante, is it? No.
No, darling. It just isn't.

[Such deplorable fatalism! A somewhat disenchanted Beatrice, perhaps?]

293
"Well, my darling –
we may at least be quite sure
that Almighty God
was not just doing it [for the *money* –]
for the material benefits, I suppose?"

294
"To have vast wealth and yet
not be spoiled by it! –
no, not in the slightest –
in fact, to be *improved* by it,
yes – yes. That's the *real* challenge, Eve."

295
– "Yes, yes. I started off
with almost wholly unrealistic
expectations – I admit that,
Adam – but isn't this in fact what a
normal human life is? No? (Didn't you?)"

296
So. Why exactly have I kept these two small pages –
torn off a calendar some thirty years ago
and only now rediscovered? Obviously, they must have been
important to me once. [Twice?] Yes. They must have been.
Very special to me once. But for how long? And why?

297
Why, Eve, should other people
be expected to take very much of an interest
in my ridiculous life? I myself
can hardly be bothered – I simply can't recall
more than the slightest ever-threatened fraction of it.

298

Not that the wider Universe out there
is keeping a safer record of it either!
No. The All is only the All, not a copy of the All.
It is not being kept, a unique treasure, safely in a box somewhere –
perhaps for a sort of Beyond-the-All to consult and peruse *ad lib.*

299

"Look, Aeream! The preserved receipt
with its old time and date
still inside the book I bought her –
which she never even bothered
to come back and reclaim!"

300

Men and women, Eve – eh? Practically none
of the most important stuff ever gets said.
Or, if said, recorded. Oh, yes; yes.
Maybe I don't know what love truly is.
But then again, darling, perhaps I do. No?

301

I don't know, I always thought –
what? –
yes, me too, I've always thought that –
what now? –
no: really? Well then, I never loved you either!

[Rather obviously, more than one person is talking here.]

302

"No, no, darling – it's just not
the sort of thing I would ever do – whereas,
with someone
as emotionally mature
as your good self, for instance – "

303
Her face changed.
Yes, I would like that
very much
very very much
she said with a slightly nervous laugh –

304
"After walking round the exhibition of sumptuous religious artefacts
for a good hour or so, O Offspring of the Heat[h]er,
we eventually strolled back to the rented flat –
where we performed various crude if mildly imaginative acts
and then quietly finished off the remainder of the food."

305
In fact, I could walk round there again right now.
Straight into that exquisite little yard of space.
A sort of darkness with enormous life
surely at some windows – at every window? – above
the doorway to a mad dream I should have followed more.

306
Instead I now find myself
rendered quite immobile
in an extremely dark space
of some sort. (Help!) Even its name
is no longer clear to me! Help!

307
"Actually, me old f★★★ing mate –
er, sorry: my incomparable Master –
I'm afraid I may even be f★★★ing well dying –
or whatever the, you know, hell it is
I am actually doing here just at f★★★ing present."

308
Oh, Danm – the rich and ludicrous variety!
Jerking about like this in almost soothing despair.
Twitching away in a suddenly compromised joy.
Or perhaps the other way about!
(Perhaps that ought even to be in the next room?)

309
But Adam – why not just escape it all and go!
What else do you need to know about it, my darling?
Yes. I may stay behind here for a while myself
mopping up any residual difficulties. Hmm.
Where do you keep the [home-made] weapons, by the way?

310
Yes. At the very least –
a look of sheer contempt
just before they shoot you.
That may perhaps do someone
some good in the [long] long run, I suppose.

311
Hello there. Am I dead yet? No?
My God, but I admire your confidence!
Why then is that always
a bit of a surprise these days? Erm.
They *are* completely destroyed, aren't they?

[Aye, verily, most mordant Ser Dauntmore, if the truth is too terrible for
you, or merely not quite to your taste, then I dare say you could always try
calling it something else. Yes. But w[ho w]ould that help in any very noble
way? You know, one does sometimes rather wonder jsut how much
(extinct) self-pity there must have been in this whole somewhat vulgar and
ridiculously over-extended Universe by now.]

312
Oh, for Heaven's sake!
Must I do all the work
myself here? Everything makes
absolute sense to me, Frank – er, Second Dan.
Yes. Well – nearly all of it, certainly!

[Frank and Dan are really just about the same name, one need hardly add, Adam. And this is, presumably, God himself talking?]

313
"A world in which holes come out of other holes!
What an absolutely *brilliant* idea, O Uniquely Great One!
I'm pretty sure I could never have managed it myself – [dear sweet
    God] –
if I had been the being left to make the practical arrangements!
(Not that that really would have been *me*, of course!)"

[Right. At a punt, this is surely some fluttering underling addressing congratulations to the Creator – massively enthusiastic and suitably humble no doubt, but, for whatever reason, evidently not quite entirely sincere – at a fairly early stage of the proceedings? (What else could it be?)]

314
Hearing his beloved wife whispering gently to him,
the Great Thinker put aside the notes he had been struggling with
since the early morning, when he had been first to wake –
turned round, kissed her head once or twice, hesitated,
made a few slight adjustments, then climbed up noisily on top of her.

[Hesitated? This is the start, surely?]

315
"But might it not even be
an all the apter image
of the humdrum if unfathomable
human condition
for all that – er, Adam?"

316
"No, Eve. In fact, I think he meant the whole Universe merely
as some sort of symbol for, you know, that, er, that unique place
where women are designed to be, er, you know, thingied – ideally,
with at least a certain amount of love – although this, I suspect
may well not have been part of the original idea as such. Whew!"

[It's not easy, is it, Son? 213 should actually follow this, I think. Of course,
the order hereabouts is all wrong. That much at least is surely obvious.]

317
But I dare say, like all really great thinkers
he was at times prey to the surely irrational fear
that he had somehow thought to jot down only
the most obvious and least truly insightful of all his countless
ideas and observations. But that's absurd, isn't it? Yes.

318
"Oh, dear God, Eve: no!
Not yet another prestigious tome
from the distinguished prize-winning literary thinker!
Quite frankly, I would rather just sit here for a while on my own
repeating the word ★★★★ to myself over and over again.

[Hmm. Look in your heart, Man, and write, indeed.]

319
In this small hotel room
in a foreign country
despite all my best resolutions
yet again I find myself thinking of something
unseen by me now for well over a year.

[Yes. I like thinking about things. But, then again, who doesn't?]

320
But nearly all of us are surely travelling
through these stations much too quickly! –
each of us attempting
[rarely with much success]
to find out the right names
as the signs hurtle by –

[Life, life, life. Need one spell everything out?]

321
"Alas, Eve, we had to bring to a sadly premature end
a rather charming and informative discussion
about certain nuances in various local words for '——'
in order to go off in good time
to a very tedious political-cultural dinner."

322
"Everything, Donq?
I hardly think so.
There's not a word about
menstruation in it,
just for a start."

323
And is it likely, I
ask myself, my
darling, that you
have absolutely
nothing to do with all this?

[Mere prose, obviously.]

324
"I am alive, Eve,
because of a ★★★★!
But then again –
in the long run
who isn't?"

[What? "In the long run"?]

325
"Thou, of course. And you.
And you, Eve, my darling.
Only at you really.
It's really only you who
can do it here, isn't it?"

326
Yet would I say, Vix,
that I had passed my days
more importantly than most?
Well, no. No. Of course I, er,
wouldn't. (Us? Us? One has one's private thoughts!)

[But then: what maniac would(n't)? This is the normal view, I rather think,
darling.]

327
A few odd times, in the routine park, sitting there
eating some transient piece of nothing near a statue
of the reasonably great scientist – [William Thomson, Lord Kelvin,
        in fact]
with her, of course. Is there ever much more to it really?
Was I ever memorably happier in my entire actual life?

[You were happy there too, Anlivia, weren't you? (Not Anvilia, obvi-
ously.)]

328
No – but can I really
have seen Eve's little amorous furrow
every night of this week –
and, for that matter, on one or two of the mornings,
while the city, like the kettle, routinely bubbled on nearby?

[This, in Latin, would presumably be a *Nonne* question rather than a *Num*
– if I'm remembering the distinction rightly.]

329
No, Lord, I'm afraid I was much too busy
doing [more or less] absolutely nothing
in the blissful company of my beloved,
erm, wife, to notice
that – erm – what? What was that?

[The entire Universe, Son. But don't worry yourself *too much* about it.]

330
I see (she's late back again!)
that yet more building/roofing work is being
carried out just across the road. My God!
And why
do I keep on [drinking] buying this bloody dreadful coffee?

331
In fact, there's really not all that much difference
between men and women, is there, Beatrice?
No. Except perhaps for, I suppose, the fact
that women can perhaps be so completely, totally, utterly
and absolutely bloody fantastic sometimes, aren't you just, my
      [angel] sweetheart?

[Such intellectual juvenilia!]

332

Or do you think I got it
unusually wrong? ([As usual?] Could we?)
Did the right person choose me?
Why do we nearly all (do we, darling?)
tend to meet the wrong people? No?

[Yes. Why do things like the Trojan War start – why do things like Cruci-
fixions and Flights and Massacres happen? – if not because we always keep
meeting the wrong sort of people? But then again, maybe you're exactly
the wrong sort of person to ask?]

333

After all, no part of all this sublime [farce] drama
has been written in advance, my dear Virgillia[n],
by some non-human Being.
(And little enough of it, indeed,
even by human beings like ourselves!)

334

And what do we know even of these [hours] houses
around us? – even the few we see? – scarcely
one point of one point of one point – probably
even much less than that! – the very [familiar] streets
we live our lives in – packed full, packed over-full, of what? –

335

All the meals being made for instance, to go
no further, at every moment of the day, in every
place – and one could always at any moment
go almost infinitely further, my dear Adam, in any
direction – no – in several directions at once –

336
"with not even the least idea, say,
of how their insides work, as if free-floating –
or what they must look like, my free-floating darling –
on they [babel babble bauble] bubble for a few decades or so
about their ridiculous eternal posthumous lives – "

337
A car in the street below
starts to sound its horn
perhaps out of anger –
while as for myself as a matter of fact I think I'm just about to –
yes! – sneeze. (Excuse me.)

338
A rather bizarre mechanism, perhaps –
but certainly a real one –
and what else is one anyway to suggest? You know,
we should have visited that little place more often
while we still had the chance. (Why not again today?)

339
"Yes. After all,
it might for instance
have been one of those *real*
wor[l]ds, might it not, Beatrice?
And then where would we all have been?"

[4, 5, 6, 7 and 8 syllables. 'Worlds' is almost certainly the right reading, whatever my late wife used to say about it. Yes. Or whoever she *really* was.]

340

Billions of years, Eve, to produce
such vastly complex creatures
capable of killing others
for all time and for such
utterly fantastical reasons!

341

Oh, History! –
fumbling as best we could
with the obvious available buttons –
(which are so rarely
the right ones, aren't they?)

[Oh, History / is basically one long weather forecast. / Can there really be
/ (I sometimes ask myself) / enough umbrellas to go round? Well?]

342

"You seek evidence
that people die and vanish,
Adam? Are corpses
not enough for you? How much
more evidence do you want?"

343

"Yes, well – nearly all of them
had extremely progressive minds, darling, I dare say.
However, they and the unprogressive ones
are alike all dead together now anyway,
I rather tend to think. Or are they perhaps not?"

[At times this Adam and Eve sound to me more like the last two human
beings than the first ones! (By the way, the previous one also sounded a bit
like God to me, if I know my voices. (Or maybe the Devil, of course.))]

344
No doubt, Leve, the most interesting of all the snippets
of passing conversation I ever heard in my life:
"Not that I ever
even for a moment
thought you would die so soon – "

["In my worst moods, I sometimes toy with I idea that life is a process of
learning that one has missed [most of] one's chances." (*Deyp*.)]

345
"Oh, darling, I'm so glad I managed to resist
the strong temptation to ring you back and say –
(yes, well –
one of two extremely cutting things
which it did for a moment occur to me to say!)"

346
Quite how many times, O Master,
do you have to f★★★ing tell us
of your absolutely wonderful compassion?
Is there any chance, do you think,
that we might otherwise miss it?

347
"Well, I don't know, do I – no doubt they are
getting on a bit in age – they are well able
to use words impressively – they feel they ought to share
the immense knowledge, the wisdom of age which they suppose
they ought to have – (but in fact don't) – so what else can they do?"

348
"As some nonentity or other once put it:
I do not particularly wish to be remembered at all –
and I completely agree with him, Odysseus.
Or her, I suppose. Well: very many must have said it,
I dare say. In which case, I agree with f★★★ing *all* of them!"

349
O I dare say at any particular moment
something final enough from elsewhere could hit the Earth –
or the Earth, for some reason, could just explode anyway
(that we could not, let us hope, work out beforehand) –
but what can we do with that? So, Eve. Just get on with it.

350
Secrets of the Universe?
Um. No thanks, Lord –
if you don't mind –
I'm a bit busy just at present –
plenty to do for the moment at least, you know? –

351
How can the whole Universe
be, as it were, a foreign country?
Except that even one's own country
is so very often, Adom,
to some extent foreign, I suppose.

352
"I am grown terrified by the thought, O Elderslie,
that all the dead who lie buried within our great hills –
brave scions of the glens of weeping! –
hearing that a new invader has broached their native land
might suddenly wake up, hesitate, then try to make a run for it."

353
"All those convincing and exquisite young creatures
who wore out and died of old age so long ago, Eve –
or who died quite impossibly young, so long ago – oh,
I still don't quite understand how it's meant to work.
[Am I meant to understand?]
But, anyway, tomorrow morning, we really must try our best [to] –

354

"Usually on such a fine morning as this – "
"Please be quiet for a moment, darling, would you?
At this particular moment I'm actually trying to think."
"Trying to think? What? How *dare* you, Adam? Yes.
Tell me. Just who the *f***** do you think you are?"

355

Oh, Eve, I know absolutely
nothing about any of my
great-grandparents either! No, not even the one
who – or so I have been confidentially told here –
was so often almost preternaturally like me as I am now.

356

"The more and more one outlives the previous great, Joseph,
the more and more one realises that their immense achievements
reduce, reduce, save for the very best of them –
and few there are of those. No. One more rather desperate, rather
        silly, ageing person,
guessing much like the rest of us – at times perhaps slightly less
        wrongly."

357

"I have just done something
extremely bloody stupid, Odysseus.
But fortunately it had nothing
to do with a piece of fruit.
There *is* that at least."

358

The road that leads you astray
may also lead you home again.
Indeed, Panaan. Indeed.
Always provided you are extraordinarily lucky
and don't drop dead on the journey.

359
"Yes. The last morning
before I have to travel back home again.
Yes. Can I really
somehow still be here in
such a dazzling, ambiguous country?"

360
"Unknowing parents
are the norm here, Stranger. Grandparents
certainly. O Unnecessary Stranger –
who are you anyway? Why
have you come here to plague us?"

[This is obviously non-existence itself talking. No?]

361
"Oh, I'm a foreigner here, Eve, I suppose.
Except, of course, that really I'm not.
All in all, it's a fairly subtle
(and largely – or merely – political) distinction.
Oh, God – look over there! Not more invaders!"

362
"I have just done something
extremely bloody stupid, Penelope.
But I felt the Gods
were almost forcing me to do it.
Do you never get that feeling yourself?"

[Well, if this isn't it, nothing is.]

363
But, Eve, of course I have time
to kiss you[r ****] again! – we have
a good ten minutes at least
before we have to set out
for this latest [completely ridiculous] [deeply impressive] [religious]
    [political] ceremony.

[I suspect this is probably not what you might think it is. Indeed, I may
even claim to know that for a fact.]

364
A final, terrible cry of "——!"
echoed throughout the Universe.
Or perhaps 'terrible'
is not quite the right word?
(But —— certainly is.)

365
Oh, what does it particularly matter
what stops it, darling? (Age. Crash.
Heart. Loss.) Something stops it –
whether it should or not. (If that
means anything [very much] at all.)

[But every generation has to discover anew – usually with utter felt disbe-
lief, for all the theoretical fore-knowledge – that it is not the one that is, at
last, going to live forever. And every description of the Infinite which
passes itself off as complete is, to that extent at least, dishonest and [infi-
nitely, my infinite Love] untrue.]

366